THE NINTH KARMAPA'S OCEAN
OF DEFINITIVE MEANING

THE NINTH KARMAPA'S OCEAN OF DEFINITIVE MEANING

by
Khenchen Thrangu Rinpoche

Oral Translation by Lama Yeshe Gyamtso
Edited, Introduced, and Annotated by Lama Tashi Namgyal

Snow Lion
Boulder

Snow Lion
An imprint of Shambhala Publications, Inc.
4720 Walnut Street
Boulder, Colorado 80301
www.shambhala.com

© 2003, 2010 by Khenchen Thrangu Rinpoche, Karme Thekchen Chöling, and Kagyu
Shenpen Ösel Chöling

9 8 7 6 5 4

Text designed and typeset by Gopa & Ted2, Inc.

Printed in the United States of America

∞ This edition is printed on acid-free paper that meets the
American National Standards Institute z39.48 Standard.
♻ Shambhala Publications makes every effort to print on recycled
paper. For more information please visit www.shambhala.com.
Snow Lion is distributed worldwide by Penguin Random House, Inc.,
and its subsidiaries.

The Library of Congrec catalogues the previous edition of this book as follows:
Thrangu, Rinpoche, 1933–
The Ninth Karmapa's ocean of definitive meaning/by Khenchen Thrangu Rinpoche;
oral translation by Lama Yeshe Gyamtso; edited, introduced, and annotated by Lama
Tashi Namgyal.
p. cm.
Translation of an oral commentary on the Ninth Karmapa's "lhan cig skyes sbyor gyi
zab khrid nges don rgya mtsho'i snying po phrin las 'od 'phro"
ISBN 978-1-55939-202-0 (paperback: alk. paper)
ISBN 978-1-55939-370-6 (paperback: alk. paper)
1. Mahāmudrā (Tantric rite) 2. Śamatha (Buddhism) 3. Vipaśyanā (Buddhism)
4. Meditation—Bka'-brgyud-pa (Sect) I. Tashi Namgyal, Lama, 1942–II. Title.
BQ7699.M34 T47
294.3'4435—dc22
2003017045

CONTENTS

INTRODUCTION

by Lama Tashi Namgyal

T HE NINTH GYALWANG KARMAPA, Wangchuk Dorje (1556-1603), wrote three definitive handbooks on how to attain the realization of mahamudra, and thus nondual, nonconceptual meditative awareness: *Pointing Out the Dharmakaya, Eliminating the Darkness of Ignorance,* and *The Ocean of Definitive Meaning.* Here we are presenting Khenchen Thrangu Rinpoche's commentary on *The Ocean of Definitive Meaning.* This text has recently been translated according to the teachings of Khenchen Tsultrim Gyamtso Rinpoche and The Dzogchen Pönlop Rinpoche by Elizabeth Callahan and published by Nitartha *international.*

In his introduction to the text, Pönlop Rinpoche writes, *"The Ocean of Definitive Meaning* contains the most detailed and direct oral instructions on mahamudra meditation ever put into writing. This extraordinary classic instruction treatise is known for its lucidity and its original Kagyü lineage style, and serves as a step-by-step personal guide to the mahamudra tradition."

The commentary of Khenchen Thrangu Rinpoche on *The Ocean of Definitive Meaning* presented here is not a systematic presentation in detail, section-by-section, of the book, but rather an introduction to its contents, emphasizing and presenting in-depth commentary on those parts of the book that Rinpoche felt would be most beneficial to those who were in attendance at the retreat where it was given. It therefore emphasizes the actual practice of mahamudra in its two stages of the mahamudra versions of shamatha (tranquility or calm abiding) and vipashyana (insight). It includes sections of commentary on pointing out the mind within stillness, pointing out the mind within movement, and pointing out mind within appearances. There is also commentary on enhancing the practice of mahamudra; on recognizing, avoiding, and dispelling hindrances or obstacles to proper practice and realization; on making progress on the path; and on the manner in which fruition manifests.

This commentary does not contain descriptions of the preliminary practices of mahamudra. For that one can refer to other sources, which are indicated in the footnotes to the commentary itself. It also does not contain actual pointing-out, which can only be received in person from a qualified guru. If one finds these teachings inaccessible because they seem to be over one's head, useful suggestions as to more preliminary approaches to spiritual practice can be found in *Shenpen Ösel* 4, no. 3 (2000): 6-7. As is the case in the study and practice of all other aspects of the teachings of tantra or vajrayana, one should practice these teachings under the guidance of a qualified guru.

These teachings are being published at the request and with the encouragement of Khenchen Thrangu Rinpoche.

᠅

The footnotes to this commentary make frequent reference to teachings published in issues of *Shenpen Ösel*. All of these references and the entirety of the teachings in which they are contained can be read and downloaded free of charge at the web site of *Shenpen Ösel*: http://www.shenpen-osel.org. Back copies of these magazines can also be ordered directly by following procedures on the web site.

Students who wish further teachings on the topics contained in this commentary can find Khenchen Thrangu Rinpoche's commentary on *Pointing Out the Dharmakaya* in a companion volume published by Snow Lion Publications.

In the course of his commentary, Thrangu Rinpoche also presents aspects of the Buddha's mahayana teachings on emptiness by way of introducing the view of mahamudra. These teachings are further illuminated by a concise two-session teaching on the progressive stages of meditation on emptiness given by Khenpo Tsultrim Gyamtso Rinpoche and published in *Shenpen Ösel* 6, nos. 1-2 (2003). In this teaching Khenpo Rinpoche makes comparisons between some of the Buddhist views and various viewpoints of various Western traditions, and offers advice on how to present the buddhadharma to various sorts of people.

᠅

The dharma teachings of the Buddha Shakyamuni have endured to the present day because, although he taught two thousand, five hundred years ago in a very different time and place, his teachings are as timely and useful today as they were then. When the dharma is studied, understood, and successfully practiced, it still provides the same kind of key, blueprint, and universal tool to understanding our own perceptions and behavior and the perceptions and behavior of others, and indeed, with increased fruition, even provides insight into the workings of the entire world with its suffering, discord, and warfare. This understanding, if it becomes profound and extensive enough, can in the end provide a remedy and an eventual end to the massive suffering we see around us. Mahamudra, which is the essence of all the Buddha's teachings, as it is taught in *The Ocean of Definitive Meaning* and in this commentary by Khenchen Thrangu Rinpoche, is the basis for such a remedy leading to the end of suffering.

According to the tradition of mahamudra, we experience all of our suffering because we misperceive reality. We can begin to understand the manner of this misperception by considering our current political situation.

At the time of this writing the United States is engaged in another terrible war. As I have watched it on television, I have found myself on one level a bit perplexed. My pre-1960s mentality, formed by an education that convinced me that America was the good guys and that American government and the American system in general were the repository of all right principle in the universe, is very impressed with and has the tendency to rejoice in the seemingly benign attitudes that one sees very often in the war faction. Though they are engaged in preemptive warfare, their manner is polite and conscientious about trying to save lives. They have spent years creating "smart weapons" to take out only hard military targets which at the same time will avoid as never before in the history of warfare the killing of innocent civilians. They slowly close the noose on Baghdad, making extensive excursions through the city with their tanks and armored weapons, not wanting to kill anybody, but wanting simply to demonstrate American presence and overwhelming military might, hoping that the enemy will then happily lay down their arms. They engage in what must be very reasonable and reassuring conversations with Iraqi generals, Islamic imams, and other elements of the Iraqi leadership, undoubtedly assuring them safety and all kinds of economic and political assistance for their cooperation with the United States' benign intention to liberate the Iraqi people from a harsh and brutal dictatorship into the blessings of liberal democracy and economic liberty.

My late 1960s mentality, on the other hand, which evolved over a seven-year career of organizing in the civil rights and anti-war movements, is a bit more cynical. To this mind, the "benign" aspect of the war party is nothing other than the sheep's clothing on the wolf. The effort to avoid both our own military casualties and the collateral casualties in enemy civilian populations is simply an effort to eliminate any opposition at home to our military actions, or at least the effectiveness of any such opposition. After all, the Vietnam War was lost in large part because of increasing opposition to the war by the American people. The fact that "body bags" has become a ver-boten expression in the military, that displays of war carnage, especially of wounded and dead American soldiers, by the American media, have been highly discouraged by the military, and that the war reportage in general is being sanitized, is evidence of the military's intense concern that a "fifth col-umn" among the American people not be opened up in this war. That the United States is spending a lot of time on the telephone and through email with the Iraqi military and other elements of the Iraqi leadership is simply evidence that the United States wishes to preserve intact as many as possible of the human resources of Iraq. These human resources will be needed after the battles to maintain internal law and order and to ensure Iraq's safety from external aggression. At the same time the US will want to preserve the cheap labor force to dig the wells and man the pumps while the United States and its friends exploit the Iraqi oil fields for their own benefit. To this rather cyn-ical mind, maintaining the myth that the United States forces are protecting these oil fields for the benefit of the Iraqi people is merely a deception they intend to get away with—and probably will get away with—on the great propaganda principle practiced by Machiavellian politicians everywhere that there is no need to tell the truth: Tell the people often enough what you want them to believe and they will believe it. When they talk about liberal democ-racy, what they are really talking about are political institutions and elections that the United States can control through strategic covert infusions of funds. Once created, these institutions and elections will ensure that the Iraqis develop a commitment to the economic liberty manifest in the free market capitalist system. And when they talk about economic liberty, what they are really talking about is de-nationalizing or privatizing the Iraqi oil industry and turning it over to the oil companies of America and its friends—all of this in the name of Iraqi freedom and the national security of the United States. The real intention of all of this is the beginning of American control over something between 54 percent and 67 percent of the total oil reserves of the world by the year 2020. In a world increasingly dependent on oil—in a world in which China, as an example, will need to get three-quarters of its oil from the Middle East by the same year—American hegemony in Iraq and in the rest of the Middle East means power and leverage in international affairs.

It would be surprising if many of these and similar ideas have not been running through the minds of other Americans, many of whom have taken sides in this conflict. But the majority of Americans in all likelihood are ter-ribly and increasingly confused. We cannot truly say that we know what's going on in all of this. We cannot really read the hearts and minds of the Iraqi people, nor, for that matter, of the American leadership. We can hear what they say, but we have been conditioned over the years not to take anything that they say at face value because they have been caught lying to us so often, especially in the area of foreign policy, which is so far removed from the daily experience of the American people that it is impossible for us to make completely informed judgments about it. We feel concerned, but do not know what to do. We want to do something, but what if we are wrong? What if we truly misunderstand the situation? Then we risk compounding the problem. It is taught in the Buddhist tradition that compassion without wisdom only leads to endless wandering through the realms of suffering of conditioned existence.

Somehow we also feel that if we just could know the "facts" ("Just the facts, Ma'am, only the facts," says Sergeant Joe Friday), we could understand the situation and would then be able to act appropriately and compassionately. But the problem is that there are no "facts." In the words of Norman Mailer, "facts" are just "intensified fantasies."

The world that ordinary beings live in is a world whose foundation is dualistic consciousness: I experience myself in here in my mind in my body perceiving something out there that is separate from me. However, what the eyes see, the ears hear, the nose smells, the body touches and feels, the tongue tastes, are none of them experienced *directly* by us. We only experience our own vague conceptualized version of what the sense organs experience. We experience actually a mental replica of the experience of the senses. This conceptual replica is merely a vague approximation of the original unconfused data of the senses that the mental consciousness has conceptualized, solidified, and projected back onto the objects and events experienced by the senses. It is that vague approximation, that replica, that we perceive and that then forms the basis for our actions of body, speech, and mind. In the words of Nagarjuna, "The phenomena that appear [through the sense organs] to the mental consciousness, the chief of them all, / Are conceptualized and then superimposed." This superimposition, which we are here calling a replica, is conditioned by all that we have experienced with like objects in the past.

If an object suddenly appears in front of us, we know by virtue of the fact that it is not rooted to the ground and can move that it is a sentient being. We know by its upright posture and its two legs, etc., that it is a human being. We know by its particular shape and its dress and its voice that it is likely to be male, for example. If our experience with males has been generally positive, at this point we will be having a generally positive perceptual experience. However, if our father beat us often, if we have been raped, or if we have been condescended to or discriminated against because of our gender, we may be having a negative perceptual experience instead; we may see a potentially aggressive and dangerous person, a potential rapist, or a male chauvinist. If we see a black-haired, slightly swarthy, heavily bearded young man with indigestion at an airport, we may instantly be afraid, assuming that we may be seeing a disgruntled, angry terrorist. In any event, we will not be seeing precisely what is in front of us.

An older Midwestern farmer with little experience of foreign affairs who sees George W. Bush on television and hears the tones and manners of his speech will very likely see a good Christian, better for his own personal reformation, and a strong and wise leader doing God's work. But a former student activist from the 1960s is more likely to see a representative of some aspect of the American ruling class, a representative of the oil cartels and of the military-industrial complex, the players of which are making and stand to make a great deal of money through this war. This latter mentality is likely to see an imperial conqueror, a cynical robber baron, intent only on an increase in American power, which will in turn ensure that rich Americans will be able to continue to exploit the world's wealth of raw materials and cheap labor for their own benefit.

But none of these conceptual imputations is conveyed to us by our senses; certainly not the words, but also not even the nondiscursive but nonetheless conceptual feelings and evaluations, the first impressions, that we experience—our sense of halo and beatific glory or our sense of fangs. They are superimposed by us onto the objects of our perceptions, which projections we then assume are the reality of what we are seeing.

If one is a born-again, evangelical Christian, and has often heard preached the scriptural revelations of the end days, with the Jews' return to their homeland, the coming of the anti-Christ, Armageddon, the rapture, and the second coming, it is not impossible that one might instantly have the feeling, even the certainty, that one is seeing that scenario taking place, and produce instant replicas or mental projections of the American leadership as Godly men and women.

As mahayana Buddhists, we have our own teachings concerning the correctness of engaging in a little harm in order to prevent a greater evil, or engaging in a little harm to create a great good. We also have our experiences and memories of the Second World War, in which a great deal of violence was perpetrated in order to eliminate what we then perceived as a much greater evil. . Seeing the relatively gentle nature of the warfare in Iraq—gentle compared with the United States' fire-bombing and nuclear-bombing of civilian populations that took millions of lives during World War II—and seeing the rapid accomplishment of objectives in Iraq and the initial jubilation of the people in the streets, we may also generate benign replicas in our minds and project them onto the American leadership and onto the events of this war. Based on these replicas, we may think that this activity involving a minimum of violence is necessary to eliminate preemptively a much more horrific suffering, and all of this we might then take as the actual facts or as the reality of what we are seeing and otherwise perceiving. But, again, none of these conceptual imputations is conveyed to us by our senses; they are superimposed by the mental consciousness onto the objects of our perceptions, which projections we then assume are actual reality.

Though it takes considerable time to express these superimpositions verbally or in writing, the basic impression of these different types of projections is conveyed to us instantaneously. The senses perceive the object, which then the mental consciousness instantly conceptualizes in a manner conditioned by all of our past experience, and superimposes this conceptualized version back onto the originally neutral data of our senses—all of this occurring so fast that we don't even notice the process, and are only left in the end with the mind's conceptual version of things that we take to be reality.

If this is what Norman Mailer means when he says that facts are merely "intensified fantasies," he is saying a very Buddhist thing. There is a kind of Rashomon effect in everything we experience. In Akira Kurasawa's movie *Rashomon,* the same events—involving an act of killing and an act of sexual intercourse—are described by four different observers, who tell four completely different versions of the events. Kurasawa deftly leaves the question of what "truly" happened unresolved. We never know. Everyone's version favors themselves. It seems obvious that there is some conscious lying going on, but also some self-deception as well. The entire movie becomes an allegory for the process of consciousness formation. Each of the raconteurs conceptualizes the data provided by his/her senses—based on their own individual past experiences of similar objects, beings, events, and tales of such events, and based on fears about what others will think and Japanese notions of honor—and then tells their story accordingly. In the same way, our mental consciousness conceptualizes the data provided by our senses and by previous moments of mental consciousness, and superimposes these conceptual replicas back onto our perceptions, which conceptual imputations we then believe with certainty are the reality of the situation. The only difference between what is going on in this latter process of consciousness formation and *Rashomon* is that the characters in *Rashomon* are at least in some degree aware that they are deceiving others, whereas the mental consciousness is not aware that it is deceiving itself.

It is important to note that not only are our recognition of the objects as such and such and our evaluation and interpretation of them a matter of our own conceptualized superimposition onto the totally neutral and nonjudgmental data of our senses, but so too is our very seeing of the data of our senses as real and solid and individuated objects, real and solid beings, and real events really taking place in a real and solid world through real time. All of these actually are the illusory and ephemeral display or radiance or light of the mind that is experiencing them, as are all the evaluations, distinctions, and judgments about them that we make. So too are our notions of past, present, and future.

People who become famous are invariably subjected to this conceptualizing and superimposing effect in a way even more dramatic than the rest of us. They are invariably seen in a multiplicity of different ways, all of which are generally different from the way they see themselves. They are adored, respected, scorned, vilified, laughed at, etc., all depending on how they are perceived by different segments of the public. How they are perceived and the names used to describe these perceptions—man or woman of God, wise statesman, strong and righteous leader, liberator, cynical politician, political hack, robber baron, invader, vicious imperial conqueror, etc.—are all simply vague projections of other people's minds, imputed by those minds to the objects of their senses, based on what they have experienced in the past. None of them are the original data of the senses. What are the facts of the matter? There are no facts. The so-called facts are all the "intensified fantasies" of the perceivers.

As our understanding of the teachings and our meditative experience of reality grow through our study and practice of Buddhism, we may have a tendency, therefore, to find ourselves politically paralyzed by this understanding and experience, which tends to diminish our reflex to make conceptual judgments As good people and citizens of advanced industrial democracies, we feel uncomfortable with this paralysis, because we would like to do something about all of the suffering that is being created. But if we cannot be sure of the facts of the matter and therefore cannot be sure of what it would be right to do, how can we do anything? We might just be making matters worse.

There is an answer to this dilemma and that answer is to cultivate awareness. What do we mean by awareness, and how is it different from dualistic consciousness? How is simply cultivating awareness going to help?

In the words of Khenpo Tsultrim Gyamtso Rinpoche:

> *Know that perception involved with the duality of perceiver and perceived is consciousness.*

Know that awareness itself, liberated from perceiver and perceived,
is primordial awareness: the dharmadhatu.

If one can transcend dualistic consciousness, thereby attaining primordial awareness, then one can see things accurately, without any conceptual projections, just as they truly are. One is tempted to say that then, having transcended "intensified fantasies," there are "facts," but these are totally nonconceptual facts that lack all the solidity that in ordinary perception we superimpose. Seeing things accurately just as they are, one can respond to things appropriately without preconceived ideas. At this level of unmistaken perception, proper and unmistakenly compassionate decision-making is decidedly possible.

Such decision-making in the dance and play of the myriad possibilities in any given situation is, then more akin to the decision-making process that takes place in the course of making aesthetic judgments than it is to following a code of conceptual morality or ideology. Such decision-making is, in fact, not at all about conceptual morality or ideology. Buddha activity, according to Lord Gampopa, "is working for the benefit of others without preconceived ideas," and conceptual morality and ideology are all sets of preconceived ideas.

But if such decision-making is only possible through transcending dualistic consciousness, what does it mean to transcend duality or dualistic consciousness? A common and quite understandable misconception of what it means is that somehow in some simplistic way we become one with all things. But this possibility, seen almost in a kind of physical sense, is a product of dualistic consciousness itself and is contravened by conventional experience. After all, even the great enlightened beings we have met through Himalayan Buddhism all seem to have their individual manifestations, which seem on the face of it to be separate from other phenomena and to function in much the same way as we do ourselves. In what way do they, and can we, transcend duality?

Transcending duality does not mean to discover that everything in some simplistic way is one; rather transcending duality means to recognize the sameness of the essential nature of all things. When we recognize the nature of all things and the sameness of that nature in all things, the activity of conceptualizing the nonconceptual experience of our senses and then superimposing such conceptualized replicas back onto the initial data of our senses is abandoned. In this nondual state in which all projections have been abandoned, direct and unmistaken insight into events and the objects of our senses spontaneously arises, while at the same time true and impartial love and compassion for the sentient beings who inhabit such events also arises.

Then we are no longer confused by our perceptions and mental replicas and can respond to events in an infallibly helpful way.

When one has become accustomed to this nondual, nonconceptual wisdom awareness, which we call original wisdom or primordial awareness, and can carry it over into all of one's daily activities, then one is able spontaneously and without conceptual contrivance to act appropriately in all situations. This level of spiritual awareness is equivalent to the awareness of buddhas, and of bodhisattvas on the eighth, ninth, and tenth bhumis. These great beings, beginning with bodhisattvas on the eighth bhumi, have completely and permanently transcended dualistic consciousness and therefore, while performing only great benefit for beings in all of their activities, no longer create karma—which arises only out of actions based on dualistic consciousness. The activities of such beings, and potentially of ourselves, are not governed and need not be governed by any conceptual reference to codes of ethics, religious principles, or political and social ideologies, etc., to be good and beneficial. Sentient beings always benefit from such activity, even if it seems to contradict conventional morality.

Therefore, since it is difficult to know who is an eighth, ninth, tenth bhumi bodhisattva, or who is a buddha, it is very often difficult to judge the activities of beings. According to the teachings of the Buddha, unless we have reached the spiritual awareness equivalent to the awareness of a first bhumi bodhisattva, it is impossible for us to judge with certainty the correctness of others' actions. Therefore, it is impossible for us to know with certainty whether the actions of the American leadership in this most recent war have been good and just and necessary, or whether at root they have been simply self-interested and rapacious.

Thus it is that those of us who have not achieved the spiritual awareness equivalent to the awareness of bodhisattvas can feel politically paralyzed. We are neither in a position to establish with certainty the "facts" of the situation, which might enable us conceptually to make good judgments concerning events and our reaction to them, nor have we attained the ability to maintain nondual, nonconceptual awareness in all of our activities, which would then enable us to act spontaneously with appropriate skillful means to contribute to the alleviation of the suffering of the beings in this war, as in all situations, and thereby also to generate the conditions for their well-being.

❧

But this does not mean that we cannot act. If we can attain nondual, nonconceptual awareness in meditation, we are engaged in profound political activity, even though we may lose this awareness during the times we are not formally meditating. (It is taught in the buddhadharma that the bodhisattva has the same essential awareness during meditation as does a buddha. The difference between them lies in the fact that the buddha's awareness in post-meditation is the same as during meditation, while a bodhisattva's awareness changes. During post-meditation the bodhisattva sees all things like an illusion, a dream, a reflection, an echo, a flash of lightning, a mirage, a magical display, a hallucination, etc.). Meditating in nondual, nonconceptual awareness, which is meditating on the dharmadhatu, immediately begins systematically to destroy in ourselves the structure of dualistic consciousness with all its attendant cognitive obscurations and emotional afflictions. From the standpoint of duality, since this dualistic consciousness also involves other sentient beings as the other pole of our duality, our activity in dissolving this consciousness has a profound impact on them as well. While our nondualistic, nonconceptual meditation is purifying our own obscurations and afflictions and thereby transforming our personal experience of others, it is also becoming a spark of buddha activity in those others. As our meditation becomes effective, the attitude of others towards us begins to change, and they themselves begin to turn inward and to search with greater conscientiousness through the stuff of their own minds and lives for spiritual solutions to their own problems. And as the power of our meditation increases, this effect reaches ever-widening concentric circles of sentient beings with whom we have karmic interdependence, which in this day and age includes not only our immediate family and friends, working associates, and local communities, but also everyone with whom we are connected through all the media of our lives.

This reality of nondual, nonconceptual awareness is reflected in the answer Kyabje Kalu Rinpoche gave Arnaud Desjardins when asked, "What is the Truth?" Rinpoche replied, "You live in illusion and in the appearance of things. There is a reality and you are that reality, but you don't know it. But if you should ever wake up to that reality, you will realize that you are nothing [empty], and being nothing [empty], you are everything. That's all." That realization is the magic elixir of truth that uncovers and inspires the manifestation of basic goodness on both sides of the dualistic equation.

In Buddhist scriptures the success of this effect and its impact on society are first described and implied in the mahayana when the ever-increasing powers of bodhisattvas are described—bodhisattvas being by definition those who in meditation can enter at will into nondual, nonconceptual awareness. First bhumi bodhisattvas, if they have renounced the life of a householder, are said to be able to enter in an instant one hundred different types of meditative absorptions, to be able to move one hundred world systems, and to be able to mature one hundred different sentient beings. These are but three of twelve sets of distinctive abilities that bodhisattvas have, beginning with the first bhumi. On the second bhumi, the number in each set of these abilities is one thousand. On the third bhumi, it reaches to one hundred thousand; on the fourth, one million. On the tenth bhumi, these numbers are described as being equal to the "billions and trillions of atoms in all the limitless buddha fields." On the bhumi of buddhahood, the numbers are said to be infinite.

If one considers even just the single quality of being able in an instant "to mature X number of sentient beings"—meaning to inspire them to increasing degrees of affection, compassion, joy, and equanimity; to pacify their emotional afflictions and to enrich them materially and spiritually; to intensify their interest in spiritual matters; to destroy their obstacles; and to inspire them to increasing introspection and wisdom—then this represents genuine political effectiveness arising exclusively out of nondual, nonconceptual meditative absorption.

In the nine-yana system of describing the Buddhist path from the standpoint of Buddhist tantra, the "political" impact of nondual, nonconceptual meditative absorption and of the skillful means that arise out of it is made very clear in the descriptions of maha yoga tantra, the seventh of the nine yanas. Yogis and yoginis who have attained the spiritual levels described in maha yoga tantra can exercise a profound effect on social groups as large as whole nation states and even far beyond. Such meditation is indeed genuine and effective political activity.

This type of political activity is far superior to ordinary political activity of any sort, no matter how well intentioned such ordinary political activity may be. Nondual, nonconceptual awareness in meditation asserts a subtle but immense spiritual influence impartially on all elements of one's experience, so that without having to make conceptual judgments and choose sides in political conflicts, one's meditation exercises a positive influence on all beings who are party to such conflicts. This positive influence is unmistaken because it is without partiality; the rain of this meditative blessing falls on the "just" and the "unjust" alike, and ultimately becomes inspiration to all of them.

Especially in such societies as the ones in which we presently live, characterized by the interdependence of highly specialized and very technical activity, it is not possible for ordinary political activity, even coming from one so powerful as the president of the United States, to govern properly all the myriad decisions of all the highly specialized individuals with totally different and mutually ununderstandable areas of expertise. And yet the technical decisions of all these myriad individuals always involve moral decisions that affect all of our lives.

For example, how many of us truly understand the activities of the Federal Reserve Board? How many of us truly understand the moral and ethical implications of all the scientific and medical research being conducted at this moment in the world? How many of us truly understand the implications and consequences of American diplomacy? How many of us truly understand the moral and ethical consequences of agricultural research? Of constantly taking minerals, chemicals, metals, and precious gems out of the earth? Of all the various activities of corporate America in general? These are but a few of the innumerable branches of human activity that take place daily and increasingly impact our lives. How can we hope to be able to judge all the decisions being made in these areas of human endeavor and engage in unmistakenly wise external political activity in the effort to control and rectify them? How many of us are *truly* qualified—even if our system as it stands made it possible—to elect a leader who can properly and compassionately preside over all these decisions? And how many leaders could possibly guide all of these decisions intelligently and compassionately?

Because of our ignorance and uncertainty in all of these highly technical situations of interdependence, the most profound and the only truly effective and unmistaken political activity is the profound spiritual influence that arises out of true, unmistaken meditative awareness, which is nondual, nonconceptual meditative awareness, which is primordial awareness, original wisdom, mahamudra and dzogchen. This spiritual influence moves the myriad decision makers, regardless of the outcome of elections and other aspects of the ordinary political and governmental process, increasingly to manifest in accordance with their own basic goodness. We cannot by any other means beneficially guide the millions and billions of incredibly important decisions that must be made constantly, instant by instant, by other people. The only way that we can move all of these individual decisions simultaneously in the right direction is through the subtle but profound influence of nondual, nonconceptual meditative awareness. In the words of Lao Tzu, "The wise person accomplishes everything by doing nothing, and the people think they did it themselves."

This "nothing," which in Buddhism would be better translated or expressed as emptiness or sunyata—is the nondual, nonconceptual wisdom awareness that is attained through the practice of mahamudra and dzogchen. This same idea is expressed in Milarepa's *Song of Mahamudra:*

At the time I'm meditating on mahamudra,
I rest without struggle in actual real being.
I rest relaxed in a free-from-wandering space.
I rest in a clarity-cradled-in-emptiness space.
I rest in awareness and this is blissful space.
I rest unruffled in nonconceptual space.
In variety's space I rest in equipoise.
And resting like this is native mind itself.
A wealth of certainty manifests endlessly.
Without even trying self-luminous mind is at work.
Not stuck in expecting results, I'm doing okay.
No dualism, no hopes and fears, Ho Hey!
Delusion as wisdom, now that's being cheerful and bright!
Delusion transformed into wisdom, now that's all right!

Milarepa sings that while meditating on mahamudra, he abides effort-lessly in the recognition of the true nature of mind and reality, which is actual real being: "I rest without struggle in actual real being." The profundity of this line rests in the description of Milarepa's "political activity," which is entirely without all the stress and strain, all the struggle and sacrifice and mental anxiety and joylessness we experience in ordinary political activity—conservative, radical, revolutionary, and otherwise—however romantically we force ourselves to regard it in order to justify our state of suffering in doing it.

Regardless of what arises in his meditation, he is subject to no fascination or fear or any kind of emotional or cognitive defilement that would cause him to wander from that recognition of actual real being into any kind of per-sonal, societal, political, religious, or even metaphysical psycho-drama: "I rest relaxed in a free-from-wandering space."

Specifically, he sees the true nature of anger and all other forms of aggres-sion and thus is not moved from that recognition by them, but instead expe-riences their transformation: "I rest in a clarity-cradled-in-emptiness space." He sees the true nature of desire and greed and all other forms of passion, is not moved from that recognition by them, and instead experiences their transfor-mation: "I rest in awareness and this is blissful space." He sees the true nature of stupidity, confusion, false conceptuality, apathy, and other forms of bewil-derment, is not moved from that recognition, and instead experiences their transformation: "I rest unruffled in nonconceptual space." No matter how these various confused mind states and emotional afflictions arise in his mind, including thoughts that might exalt him or humiliate him, he rests in perfect equanimity, seeing the equality or one-taste-nature of all mental experiences when the mind unfailingly rests in their true nature as they arise: "In variety's space I rest in equipoise." Resting like this, he says, is native mind itself—the actual true nature of mind and everything that arises in it or from it.

While describing the nature and joy of mahamudra, which is nondual, nonconceptual meditative awareness, Milarepa also describes the utter certainty he has in the truth, virtue, and efficaciousness of resting in this state of meditative awareness, when he sings, "A wealth of certainty manifests endlessly. Without even trying self-luminous mind is at work."

The expression of efficaciousness is a bit hidden by the translation in the words, "Without even trying self-luminous mind is at work," which really means, "Without even trying, self-luminous mind is accomplishing buddha activity." Buddha activity includes pacifying, enriching, magnetizing, and destroying— pacifying emotional affliction, and therefore conflicts of all sorts, including warfare; both materially and spiritually enriching sentient beings; magnetizing or attracting beings to spiritual paths and causing them to see the superiority of true spiritual paths to the samsaric things they are engaged in; and destroying obstacles, both spiritual and societal, to further human development.

Seen from another perspective, self-luminous mind is also at work in removing the cognitive and emotional obscurations that block the natural expression of affection, compassion, joy, and equanimity inherent in the true nature of mind in all beings, regardless of how confused they may currently be. And as nondual, nonconceptual meditative absorption removes these obscurations with ever-increasing speed and ever-increasing power, self-luminous mind is increasingly at work producing not only the manifestation of love in our world, but the power and efficaciousness of love in our world; not only in producing the manifestation of compassion in our world, but the power and efficaciousness of compassion in our world; not only in generating increasing wisdom and skillful means in our world, but the power and efficaciousness of wisdom and means.

This is genuine political effectiveness, and is quite subversive in nature, because instead of trying to impose these results on a reluctant world, this approach inspires others to generate these results of their own accord in their own lives and in realms of their own experience. "The wise person accomplishes everything by doing nothing [i.e., by resting in nonconceptual, nondual wisdom], and the people think they did it themselves."

The nondual, nonconceptual meditative absorption of mahamudra and dzogchen is truly compassionate political activity, and is the source of great joy and psychological sustenance. In the words of Khenchen Thrangu Rinpoche:

"Usually we regard compassion as a state of misery, because you see the sufferings of others and you cannot do anything about it, and that makes you miserable. But the compassion that arises through the recognition or realization of mahamudra is not a state of misery; it is actually a state of great bliss.

"As is said in the *Aspiration of Mahamudra,* 'At the moment of kindness, emptiness arises nakedly.' The compassion that arises out of mahamudra ensues upon the recognition of emptiness, but at the very moment at which compassion arises, there is also further experience of emptiness itself. Which is to say that at the very moment compassion arises, that very compassion and any sense of a dualistic split between the subject and object of that compassion are co-emergently seen as empty, and the positive qualities inherent in the natural state are spontaneously present.

In particular, because of the realization from which this compassion ensues, you see exactly how beings could, can, and will be liberated. You see exactly how you could help beings and exactly how beings can come to the same realization. Therefore it is not a compassion of hopelessness; it is a compassion of great optimism.

"While, from one point of view, we would consider compassion a type of sadness or characterized by sadness, in the case of the compassion of mahamudra, because of the tremendous confidence that your realization gives you, confidence not only in your own realization, but in the possibility of realization on the part of all beings, then compassion is also regarded as bliss."

This is genuine unmistaken political activity.

Those of us who have an inspiration toward this path, for the sake of all sentient beings—not to mention for the sake of our children and grandchildren and their future generations—have a responsibility, therefore, to engage in such meditation if we can, or to bend our efforts toward cultivating such meditative awareness if presently we cannot.

How do we even know that such spiritual influence actually does exist and can be exercised? The evidence of the existence of such profound spiritual influence is our own personal experience of the great spiritual beings of Tibet whom we have met and with whom we have studied. We have all sat in rooms listening to their teachings and receiving their empowerments. Under such conditions, we have experienced our anxieties and physical discomforts and sufferings dissolving. We have experienced our consciousnesses being transformed. At the very least we have all experienced our negativity dissolving and have experienced the growth of positive qualities in the presence of such beings. Therefore, we know from personal experience that such spiritual influence exists. Those who have exercised it in our lives, these same great beings, have made it unceasingly clear to us that we too are capable of liberating this same spiritual influence from the original wisdom that lies temporarily obscured in our own minds.

Reading this, one might reasonably argue, "But I am not a buddha; I am not an enlightened bodhisattva. I cannot enter at will into nondual, nonconceptual meditative awareness. When I look at my mind, all I see is a mess. And at the rate I am going, I will never attain such nondual awareness."

To these frequently occurring thoughts, the only appropriate answer—if we truly and genuinely wish to become politically effective and help save the world from its potentially self-destructive course—is that we can no longer afford the mental laziness of such low self-esteem. We must continue to fit ourselves into this path of mental and spiritual development and to exert ourselves in it. Even the least effective effort that we make in meditation has a positive influence on our world. Our reliance on the three jewels and the three roots, our cultivation of bodhicitta, our recitation of mantra, our practice of shamatha and vipashyana, and our dedications and prayers—especially if at the time of doing them we visualize ourselves and all other sentient beings engaged simultaneously in these activities—also collectively inspire the world of our experience in a positive direction. All such efforts also, of course, bring about the accumulation of merit and wisdom and are conducive to the recognition of the true nature of things and the ability to rest in nondual, nonconceptual meditative awareness.

One might also grow despondent about the possibility of personally developing nondual, nonconceptual meditative awareness as an effective approach to politics and social change, given the speed at which world events unfold and the power of their potential destructiveness. If so, one should remember the words of Kyabje Kalu Rinpoche to Lama Norhla Rinpoche, that if one has concentration and the willingness to make the effort, "Buddhahood is not that far away." When Kalu Rinpoche was leaving us in three-year retreat in Wappingers Falls in upstate New York in 1986, he told us that in the time of one of the Karmapas, the Karmapa and his monks used to travel around Tibet like nomads, living in tents. They would pitch their camp in one locality, practice there for a time, teach the dharma to the local people, and then move on to the next locality. During that time, the lamas and monks would practice the guru yoga of the Eighth Karmapa four times per day, and every day someone would attain siddhi or stable realization. Also, if one reads the biographies of the eighty-four Indian mahasiddhas, one will find that twelve years was most frequently cited as the period of time required for their attainment of enlightenment, and the vast majority of them had other full time occupations in the world. And Lama Norhla Rinpoche also commented that it was not unusual in Tibet for practitioners to attain siddhi in their second three-year retreat. Surely, although our societies are vastly more complex and powerful and speedy today, it is not impossible for us to emulate these examples. The point, in the words of Milarepa, is to "make haste slowly," but nonetheless to make haste.

If one thinks that the present responsibilities of one's life will not allow one to make such an effort in this lifetime, then one should remember that a journey of a thousand miles begins with a single step, continue to make efforts, and especially continue to generate the aspiration to attain nondual, nonconceptual meditative awareness in the future.

And then be fearless, remembering that the phenomena of our perceptions are merely mind, that mind itself is empty of inherent existence, that this mind continually arises in both positive and negative ways spontaneously in accordance with our own karma, and that ultimately whatever arises is self-liberated. The solidity and realness of events, our attachments to certain outcomes, our fear of others, and the seeming ineluctability of suffering are all projections of our own minds, and do not really exist, neither in the various solidified ways that we imagine, nor in any ultimate, essential sense. It is possible, and ultimately the most valuable thing that we can do politically as well as spiritually, to change the nature of our perceptions in accordance with this understanding. It is important for us not only to know the truth, but also to become the truth.

"Before meditating," teaches Thrangu Rinpoche, "before recognizing things to be as they are, you will have seen the radiance of this mind as solid external things that are sources of pleasure and pain. But through practicing meditation, and through coming to recognize things as they are, you will come to see that all of these appearances are merely the display or radiance or light of the mind which experiences them."

Regardless of where we are—in this life, in the bardo between death and rebirth, in the next life, in war and in peace—what we experience is "merely the display or radiance or light of the mind which experiences." Therefore, if we address the problems in our minds and cultivate the recognition of the true nature of mind and reality, we will also be cultivating the basis of happiness and liberation in all of those circumstances.

To recognize this true nature is true and genuine political activity. And regardless of how far along the spiritual path we are, to bend our efforts in the direction of this recognition is the most valuable thing that we can do now, as it has, in fact, always been. Nondual, nonconceptual meditative awareness is now, has always been, and will always be the basic inspiration and wellspring of all human evolution. The sooner we attain it, and especially if great numbers of us attain it, the sooner, to paraphrase Chatral Rinpoche, we will eliminate—root, branch, and leaf—even the names of those dark forces who hate others and the teachings; the sooner we will spread vast happiness and goodness over this fragile planet; and the sooner we will be able, with all strife gone, to be busy only with the dance of pleasure, the dance of joy! This is something we definitely can do.

THE NINTH KARMAPA'S
OCEAN OF DEFINITIVE MEANING

Khenchen Thrangu Rinpoche

1 FIRST ONE TAMES THE MIND WITH THE PRACTICE OF TRANQUILITY

At the Chehalis Healing Centre near Agassiz, British Columbia, in July of 2002, the Very Venerable Khenchen Thrangu Rinpoche led a mahamudra retreat, at which time he gave instructions on The Ocean of Definitive Meaning. *Rinpoche gave his instructions and commentary in Tibetan; these were orally translated by Lama Yeshe Gyamtso.*

I WOULD LIKE TO BEGIN by welcoming all of you here and by expressing my sincerest appreciation to everyone for giving me the opportunity to share this time with you, and especially for giving me this opportunity to discuss mahamudra. We will be studying *The Ocean of Definitive Meaning*,[1] the longest of what are considered to be the three greatest texts of mahamudra instruction. As many of you know, this text has now been translated into English. So I am delighted to be able to offer you instruction in this text, which you will thereafter be able to study to your benefit.

Let us chant the lineage supplication, and since the realization of mahamudra requires faith and devotion, please chant the supplication with as much faith and devotion as you can muster.

[Rinpoche and students chant:]

Supplication to the Takpo Kagyus

Great Vajradhara, Tilo, Naro,
Marpa, Mila, Lord of Dharma Gampopa,
Knower of the Three Times, omniscient Karmapa,
Holders of the four great and eight lesser lineages—
Drikung, Taklung, Tsalpa—these three, glorious Drukpa and so on,
Masters of the profound path of mahamudra,
Incomparable protectors of beings, the Takpo Kagyu,

I supplicate you, the Kagyu gurus.
I hold your lineage; grant your blessings so that I will follow
    your example.

Revulsion is the foot of meditation, as is taught.
To this meditator who is not attached to food and wealth,
Who cuts the ties to this life,
Grant your blessings so that I have no desire for honor and gain.

Devotion is the head of meditation, as is taught.
The guru opens the gate to the treasury of oral instructions.
To this meditator who continually supplicates the guru,
Grant your blessings so that genuine devotion is born in me.

Awareness is the body of meditation, as is taught.
Whatever arises is fresh—the essence of realization.
To this meditator who rests simply without altering it,
Grant your blessings so that my meditation is free from conception.

The essence of thoughts is dharmakaya, as is taught.
Nothing whatever but everything arises from it.
To this meditator who arises in unceasing play,
Grant your blessings so that I realize the inseparability of samsara
    and nirvana.

Through all my births may I not be separated from the perfect guru
And so enjoy the splendor of dharma.
Perfecting the virtues of the paths and bhumis,
May I speedily attain the state of Vajradhara.

This supplication was written by Pengar Jampal Zangpo. The last stanza is a
traditional verse of aspiration.
Translated by the Nalanda Translation Committee, slightly amended by the
KSOC Translation Committee.

People in the West are very fortunate in general nowadays because of the
flourishing of the buddhadharma, but even more fortunate because of the
serious and authentic interest in the Buddha's teachings found nowadays in
Western countries. This involves the presence of two conditions: the external or environmental condition of the availability of these teachings in your

countries, and the individual or personal condition, which is your own individual faith and openness to the teachings. The coming together of these two conditions is how many of you are making your lives most meaningful. But in all of this, what is of perhaps the greatest or most particular significance is that Western practitioners in general are seriously and genuinely interested in the practice of meditation, which is the most important feature of the Buddha's teachings. Of course, we can speak of the two accumulations, the conceptual accumulation of merit and the nonconceptual accumulation of wisdom, but even when we do so, we have to keep in mind that the ultimate purpose of the conceptual accumulation of merit is to lead to the nonconceptual accumulation of wisdom. Finally, we must accept that the true nature of the path (whether it takes the form of mahamudra practice, or the great middle way (madhyamaka), or the great perfection (dzogchen)) comes down to taming your own mind. And because you recognize this priority in practice, you are particularly fortunate.

Our text, *The Ocean of Definitive Meaning,* is divided into three main sections, the preliminaries and the two aspects of the main practice of mahamudra, which are tranquility[2] and insight.[3] The preliminaries here are divided into three groups, called the common, the uncommon, and the particular or special preliminaries. The first two sets of preliminaries, especially, have already been explained extensively by many great teachers, and many students have already practiced these assiduously.[4] Therefore, I am not going to talk about the preliminary practices. I will begin with an explanation of the mahamudra practices of tranquility and insight.

Nevertheless, before I do so, I feel I should make a few remarks about the role of the preliminaries in mahamudra practice. It is by no means the case—in other words, it is not true—that if you have not completed the preliminary practices you are somehow unfit to hear mahamudra teachings. That is not true. On the other hand, it is also not the case that these practices are unnecessary. They do serve very specific purposes, and therefore, they should not be neglected. So, if you have done the preliminary or ngöndro practices, I congratulate you, and I remind you that you are very fortunate in having done so. I urge you to continue to practice them, because these practices will definitely continue to help your cultivation of mahamudra meditation. Even though you may have completed the cycle of preliminary practices one time, if you repeat them, you will find that there is even more to be gained from these practices on a second visit. Among them, the four common preliminaries are necessary from the very start, because they are how we can discover a genuine inspiration for the practice of dharma to begin with. The uncommon preliminaries are important because they are the most effective way to cultivate the two accumulations and purify or remove the various obscurations in preparation for mahamudra practice. So therefore, please do these preliminary practices as much as you can. It is appropriate to do the preliminaries after receiving mahamudra instruction. It is also appropriate to do them if you have been instructed in them and have not yet received mahamudra instruction. You should not think that, having received mahamudra instruction, or having completed the preliminary practices once, that you can discard them. You should not think, "I am a mahamudra practitioner, I do not need that stuff anymore," because in fact you do continue to need them and they remain of great value. Nevertheless, having said that, I am not going to discuss the preliminaries further, and I will begin to present the main practices of tranquility and insight.

The particular format of instruction which characterizes the Kagyu tradition is two-fold: there is the path of liberation, which is mahamudra, and the path of method, which is the Six Dharmas of Naropa.[5] In the history of our tradition, various holy beings have used these two methods or formats of practice in different ways. Some have combined their practice and attained awakening; some have practiced only the Six Dharmas of Naropa—the path of method—and attained awakening; and some have practiced only mahamudra and attained awakening. Therefore, from a Kagyu point of view, we would say that any of these three ways of practice is okay. In this particular context, our text, *The Ocean of Definitive Meaning*, does not present the path as a combination of mahamudra and the Six Dharmas, but as the cultivation of mahamudra itself. Therefore, the whole structure of our text is based on how someone who purely practices mahamudra would proceed from the very beginning of their practice until they reached the citadel of the dharmakaya, which in mahamudra terminology is called the state of no meditation.

This book, *The Ocean of Definitive Meaning*, was previously unavailable in English, but now, as a result of the flourishing of the teachings in these countries, it is now available. Since it is such a valuable source text for your practice of mahamudra, I urge you to study and read it assiduously. I am going to operate under the assumption that you will be studying the text. Therefore, in order to make it practically available to you, I am going to attempt during the next eight days to explain the complete practice of tranquility and insight from the standpoint of mahamudra. This means that I will have to summarize this rather long text rather than go through it word by word.

In this text, the practice of tranquility meditation is said to have two aspects: the physical technique and the mental technique. The physical technique is the meditation posture, which here is explained as the seven dharmas of Vairochana.[6] I think that you must all have heard a great deal of instruction in meditation posture already, and so I feel it is not necessary for me to present it here again and am going to move on to the mental technique.

With regard to the practice of meditation in general and of tranquility meditation in particular, in the sutras we find the statement, "Utterly tame your own mind; that is the Buddha's teaching." We can infer from this that the fundamental or overriding purpose of all dharma practice is to tame our minds. The only distinctions we can make within that injunction are among the methods which are used to do so. In the practice of mahamudra two methods are used. First one tames the mind with the practice of tranquility, and then with the practice of insight. Therefore, we need to begin with the practice of tranquility.

In order to provide support and background for the practice of mahamudra, the Third Gyalwang Karmapa, Rangjung Dorje, wrote three books. The longest one of them, called *The Profound Inner Meaning*, is actually generally regarded as a source book or background reference manual for the Six Dharmas of Naropa, rather than as a source book or reference manual for mahamudra. However, the other two, called the two little books of Rangjung Dorje for the simple reason that they are both quite short, were written to provide background and understanding for the meditation practice of mahamudra itself. The names of these two books are *Distinguishing between Consciousness and Wisdom* and *An Explanation of the Essential Nature*.

Now, while these books are quite short as books go, they are nevertheless extremely profound. Their purpose, as I mentioned, is to explain how the mind works so that you understand it well enough to proceed with the practice of mahamudra. Therefore, a background is presented for both the practice of tranquility and the practice of insight. According to Rangjung Dorje's explanation in *Distinguishing between Consciousness and Wisdom*, what we call mind, which in general is that which practices meditation, consists of eight functions or eight consciousnesses. Among these it is the sixth consciousness, referred to as the mental consciousness, which practices tranquility. The first six consciousnesses are the eye consciousness, the ear consciousness, the tongue consciousness, the nose consciousness, the body consciousness and the mental consciousness. Of these the first five are sense consciousnesses. Therefore, their ability or capacity is limited to mere experience, which means they are not conceptual; they simply experience their individual objects. Therefore, the eye consciousness sees, the ear consciousness hears, the nose consciousness smells, the tongue consciousness tastes, and the body consciousness feels. None of them are in and of themselves capable of any kind of judgment, appraisal, or conceptualization. Therefore, none of these five consciousnesses are involved in the act that we call tranquility meditation.

Then, we also have the seventh consciousness, which is the afflicted consciousness or the klesha consciousness, and the eighth consciousness, which is called the all-basis or alaya consciousness. These two are also not involved in the practice of tranquility meditation.

The problem that is dealt with in tranquility meditation—and therefore the basis, or we could say, the subject of that meditation—is the arising or occurrence of thoughts, which happens in and to the sixth consciousness. Since tranquility meditation is a process of bringing the sixth consciousness, the mental consciousness, to a state of stability, it is, therefore, the sixth consciousness that performs tranquility meditation and that is primarily affected by it. Through the growing stability of tranquility meditation the mental afflictions are somewhat weakened and pacified.

This is not to say that all functions of the sixth consciousness are regarded as negative. Some of them are negative, some of them are virtuous, and some of them are neutral, but all of them involve some kind of conceptuality: the concepts of good and bad, likes and dislikes, and so on. It is because of the presence or arising of thoughts and the concepts borne by thoughts that our minds are unpacified.

Now, because the sixth consciousness is in this way conceptual, it is regarded as bewildered or confused. In this case bewilderment or confusion is meant literally, because it is the sixth consciousness that mistakes or confuses one thing for another. For example, it is the sixth consciousness that mistakenly identifies an object of external perception, such as a form, with the concept or linguistic term or word which is used to describe that form, and takes these two things to be one, when in fact they are not one. So, the sixth consciousness, which in that way is bewildered and conceptual, generates coarse concepts—thoughts that are evident and active.

Now, how does this occur? The sixth consciousness, which is referred to in the context of the discussion of the arising of thought as the principal mind, is, from one point of view, a principal mind and, from another point of view, an environment within which thoughts arise. When thoughts arise, they arise as though they were a retinue of this principal mind, which is their projector; but because they are perceived by the sixth consciousness, it may be helpful also to think of them as arising within it.

The thoughts that arise can be categorized in different ways—for example as the fifty-one mental arisings,[7] and so on. Now, it is for this reason among others that in the practice of the generation stage, deities are depicted in some of the ways that they are. For example, in the generation stage practice of the peaceful and wrathful deities one visualizes in one's heart the five male and five female buddhas in their peaceful forms, in which they represent the consciousness itself or the principal mind, while the coarse thoughts that are generated by that mind are in the context of the same visualization viewed as the fifty-eight wrathful deities visualized as being inside one's brain. The iconography of the wrathful deities represents the coarseness and the energy of the thoughts that can arise within the principal mind. And the iconography of the peaceful deities represents the fact that there is the possibility of these coarse thoughts subsiding into a state of tranquility or peace within the principal mind itself. As we know from our own experience, the various thoughts and other mental arisings—the fifty-one, and so forth, that arise within the sixth consciousness—in a physical sense occur within our brains, and that is why they are depicted in that way.

Also, if we consider the iconography of Vajrayogini, we see that she wears a long necklace of fifty-one freshly severed human heads. These freshly severed human heads do not represent human heads; they represent thoughts, and the number fifty-one is the number of types of mental arisings or samskaras that can occur within the sixth consciousness. But the nature of all these mental functions, of all the eight consciousnesses, in fact, is the five wisdoms, which in their nature are not inherently deluded or conceptual. So therefore, the five wisdoms are represented by five skulls which adorn her tiara. Now, the dryness of the skulls represents the absence of conceptual bewilderment in the nature of the mind's functions, and the wetness of the freshly severed heads represents the presence of conceptual bewilderment, which is to be cut through. As for how we cut through this conceptual bewilderment, there are many different ways of doing so, but in the context of mahamudra the method taken is neither the practice of the generation stage nor the practice of the completion stage,[8] but the direct approach of tranquility meditation which allows these concepts and thoughts to be pacified naturally within the sixth consciousness.

So in general, when we talk about the mind that meditates, we are referring to the sixth consciousness. The sixth consciousness somehow never stops, but while it never stops, and in that sense appears to go on functioning through time, its defining characteristic, indeed the defining characteristic of the mind itself as a whole, is cognitive lucidity—the capacity to know, the capacity to experience. And because that is what never stops, that cognitive lucidity, therefore, this unceasing or continuous quality of mind would in no way need to be a substantial entity. What never stops is not itself substantial. Therefore, the mind is not a solid and dead thing like a stone.

Lacking substantiality, it does not have the coarse substantial existence of something like a stone. Also, because of its insubstantiality, it is possible to change how it functions. So the starting point of the practice of tranquility meditation is the beginning of this process of changing the mind and pacifying the functions of the sixth consciousness.

In this presentation, there are two aspects to the mental technique of the practice of tranquility—the general point and particular methods. The general point here is stated as follows: "Do not prolong the past. Do not beckon the future. Rest evenly in cognitive lucidity that is without conceptualization." Now you will all be getting this book, so you will find this instruction in the book, but just so you have it right now, the basic instruction is, "Do not prolong the past. Do not beckon the future. Rest evenly in cognitive lucidity that is without conceptualization."

The first point is, "Do not prolong the past." Prolonging the past here means thinking about the past or recollecting the past. When we recollect the past, one of two things happens. If we recollect a pleasant aspect of the past, then we become excited. If we recollect an unpleasant event or aspect of the past, then we experience regret. In either case, whether we are disturbed by excitement or regret, we are distracted and are not aware of the present. So here, the first point in the practice of tranquility is to relax your mind by letting go of the past.

The second point concerns thinking about the future. What is meant by "beckoning the future" is simply thinking about the future. Whether or not we are capable in any given situation of accurately imagining the future, we think about it a great deal. Thinking about the future is fine and, indeed, necessary in post-meditation,[9] but during the practice of meditation, for the sake of uncontrived awareness, we also let go of the future. So the second point is not to speculate about the future.

Now, if you stop thinking about the past and you stop thinking about the future, what remains? You might imagine, since thoughts by their nature tend to be about the past and the future, that no cognitive function whatsoever would remain in the mind, and that your mind, therefore, would become like a dead lump of stone. In fact, this does not occur. The mind's cognitive lucidity does not depend upon thinking for its existence. You can remain in a state of cognitive lucidity even when you are not thinking about either the past or the future. So here the instruction is to remain in that cognitive lucidity that is independent of thinking about either the past or the future and to do so in a way that is free of any kind of conceptualization. Initially, when you try to do this, you can do it only briefly. As we will see later on in the text, traditionally there are enumerated nine stages to the cultivation of tranquility. In the first stage, called placement, your mind can rest in this state only briefly. In the second, called additional placement, it can rest in this state somewhat longer, and so on, as we will see in detail later. In any case, in this practice you rest in the direct awareness or experience of the present moment without conceptualizing it.

So within the second point of the practice of tranquility, the mental technique, we saw that there were two parts: the general technique or general point and the particular techniques or particular methods. What I have just presented is the general technique or general point of the mental technique for the practice of tranquility meditation. Following that, and making up the bulk of the text's presentation of tranquility, are particular techniques or particular methods, classified according to the experience of the teachers of the Kagyu tradition into three groups of techniques.

These groups of techniques are classified or divided according to what level of practice and practice experience for which they are appropriate, and are called "getting hold of it when you have not gotten hold of it," "stabilizing it when you have gotten hold of it but have not stabilized it," and "progressing when you have stabilized it but have not progressed beyond that." Each of these groups contains several techniques within it.

When you begin to practice meditation, the first thing you have to do is to get hold of the basic idea of what you are doing, and that is what is meant here by getting hold of it when you have not gotten hold of it, grasping it when you have not grasped it. This corresponds to our effort to begin really to understand through practice what meditation is. In the beginning we do not know what it is. Our minds do not stay put and we are not really sure what we are doing. So the first body of techniques is designed to enable a beginning practitioner to get hold of or grasp the fundamental process of meditation.

Then, once you know how to meditate, and you have grasped the basic process, you have to use the practice of meditation to actually develop stability within your mind. So, for that purpose, the second class of techniques is provided, which is called how to stabilize it when you have grasped it but have not yet stabilized it.

And then finally, once you have generated some stability in your mind, you need to progress further. Therefore, there is the third set of techniques, how to progress when you have stabilized the mind and the practice of meditation.

Now, in terms of the first of these, grasping it when it is as yet ungrasped, while we may know theoretically that the nature of our mind is emptiness and therefore has no substantial characteristic on which we can really fixate, it is very hard to rest in that. So in the beginning, especially, there is a need for some kind of a technique or focus. Therefore, within the first of these three classifications, grasping it when it is ungrasped, there are again three sections. Of these, the first and the easiest to perform is resting the mind on a conceptual focus, an intentionally entertained or maintained conceptual focus. But that is not enough; eventually one has to transcend that approach. Therefore, there is the second section, resting the mind without conceptual focus. And finally, there is the third, resting the mind on the breathing. So, within the first of the three sections, there are again three.

Now, within resting the mind on a conceptual focus, there are two sections [laughter]: resting the mind on an external focus, and resting the mind on an internal focus. And we are going to stop there for this morning.

[Thrangu Rinpoche and students dedicate the merit:][10]

> *Unborn, eternal, self-arising dharmakaya*
> *Arises as the miraculous kayas of form;*
> *May the three secrets of the Karmapa be stable in the vajra nature*
> *And may his limitless buddha activity spontaneously blaze.*

> *Splendor of the Teachings, Venerable Karma Lodro, may you remain*
>   *steadfastly present.*
> *Your qualities of the glorious and excellent dharma increase to fill space.*
> *May your lotus-feet always be stable,*
> *And may your buddha activity of teaching and practice blaze in all*
>   *directions.*

> *By this merit, may all attain omniscience.*
> *May it defeat the enemy, wrong-doing.*
> *From the stormy waves of birth, old age, sickness, and death,*
> *From the ocean of samsara may I free all beings.*

2 GRASPING THE MIND THAT HAS NOT BEEN GRASPED

THIS MORNING we saw that, based upon the practical experience of the teachers of our tradition, the practice of tranquility meditation has been divided into different sets of instructions, which are designed to enable students gradually to enhance their practice. Within the first category, grasping it, which here refers to the mind when it has not been grasped, the first set of instructions relies upon a conceptual focus, and the first section of those instructions includes techniques that make use of an external focus for support. The use of an external focus is further divided into two in this text: the use of an impure, which means mundane, support and the use of a pure, which means sacred, support. The first of these, the use of a mundane support, is also divided into two, the use of a gross or coarse mundane support and the use of a fine or subtle mundane support.

Within all of these subdivisions the first technique is grasping the mind when it has not yet been grasped, using a conceptual focus that is an external coarse mundane support. This technique involves simply directing your attention to whatever you naturally see in front of you. It could be a column or a wall; whatever it is, you simply rest your mind on the visual experience of that object of visual perception. The idea is to maintain a bare perception or experience of the object. You do not think about it or consider it in anyway. This technique is presented first because it is the easiest.

The second technique is getting hold of the mind using a subtle or fine support. Here, rather than simply looking at whatever happens to be in front of you, you select an object that is physically small and place it in front of you, using this neutral but physically small object as a smaller or more concentrated focus for the mind. Because the object is smaller, one needs to pay some attention to exactly what focusing the mind on the object does and does not mean. Your effort is put into not losing track of the object's presence in front of you, which means you do not forget it or become distracted to something other than the object. However, you also do not try to force your mind to rest on the object with tension, nor do you analyze the object or consider

33

its color, its shape, its identity, and so on. You simply hold your mind to the bare visual experience of the object. In order to do this, your mind must not be held too tightly. You have to allow your mind to settle on the object. It is a process of relaxing the mind into the bare perception of the object, not of forcing the mind into such a perception. Now, these two techniques—using a coarse or gross support and using a fine or subtle support—are both called "using an impure support," because the supports are neutral; they are not sacred or special in anyway.

The next technique taught is a variation of the preceding techniques, but it introduces the aspect of sacredness. This is done in order to make use of the force of your faith as a power in meditation and in order to allow the meditation simultaneously to serve the purpose of the accumulation of merit. Specifically, because it is taught in many sutras that recollection of the Buddha's form brings many benefits and is therefore an important technique of tranquility meditation, the main practice of focusing on a supermundane or sacred support is to direct your attention to an image of the Buddha, which you have placed in front of you within your line of vision.

What all three of these techniques have in common is that they tether the mind to an external support of some kind. The reason that techniques sharing this common element are presented in the beginning is that we have the habit of directing or turning our minds outward. Therefore, these techniques are easier and more natural for us as beginners.

The next technique is a further development, which does not involve directing the mind outward, but directing the mind inward. It is called grasping the mind using an internal focus. Here the internal focus is not an object that is physically present to be physically seen but something that you visualize within your body. The technique is to visualize in the center of your body at the level of your heart a small eight-petaled lotus flower. Resting on top of the center or calyx of that flower you visualize one of several things, and you have a choice here. One suggestion is to visualize your yidam or the deity on which you meditate. If you are used to visualizing a yidam and find that easy and inspiring, then you may do so. Alternatively, you may visualize your root guru or any lineage guru. If you feel that those visualizations are too demanding because of the details involved in their appearances, then you may visualize a small but brilliant sphere of light resting on top of the center of the lotus flower. In this case, it is still recommended that you think that, while the sphere of light appears in that form, it is in essence either your root guru or your yidam. In this practice you maintain your visualization as best you can, focusing your mind on it as one-pointedly as possible, so that you do not forget it or lose track of it. Because this meditation involves an internally directed focusing of the mind, it further develops the mind's ability to bring the mind to rest, the cultivation of which was begun in the preceding techniques.

At this point, four methods have been presented. Three of them are focused on an external object, and one is focused on an internal visualization or imagined object, but all four of these techniques have in common that they involve grasping the mind through tethering it to some conceptual focus or another.

The second category of tranquility meditation techniques is grasping the mind without focus, holding the mind in a state free of conceptual focus. The technique presented here makes use of the five elements: earth, water, fire, air, and space. The aspect of the five elements which is significant here is the distinction among them between coarse and subtle. It is held that the element earth is the coarsest; water is more subtle than earth; fire more subtle than water; air more subtle than fire; and space, which is held in this context to be nothing whatsoever, the subtlest. Now, there are different ways this technique has been taught. Sometimes it involves a process of dissolving or collapsing into oneself, and sometimes it involves a process of expanding and dissolving outwardly. Here it is presented as a process of expanding outwardly. When you begin the technique, you think or imagine that you are present within the mandala of earth. "Within" here means that you adopt the center of the mandala of earth as your perspective, but you do not imagine your physical body as being present physically within the mandala. You simply feel that you are within it. To say that the mandala of earth is to be visualized as a cube is misleading. It is a square with three dimensions, that has some thickness, but it is not completely symmetrical like a symmetrical cube.[11] It is visualized as being made of yellow light. So you visualize yourself as being in the midst of this truncated cube of yellow light, which is the mandala of earth, as though you were, for example, inside a room. You think that outside that is the mandala of water, which is a quite thick disc of white light. (Rinpoche did not say this, but it is kind of like a hockey puck. He gave me permission to say this, just so you get the dimensions right.) So, just as the earth mandala is your dwelling, so to speak, the water mandala is the dwelling or the container for the earth mandala, and is also seen as being more subtle than it. In the same way, outside of and containing the water mandala is the fire mandala: a triangle of red light, again having thickness so that it can contain the water mandala. Then finally outside of and containing the fire mandala is the mandala of wind: a semicircle of green light, also having thickness so that it can contain the fire mandala. In the context of this meditation the mandala of space, which is the container for wind or air, is thought of as empty space, as not having any kind of shape or form.

So you visualize all of that, and once it has been visualized, you then think that the mandala of earth, which is the innermost part of the visualization and the basis of your perspective, dissolves outward into the mandala of water. Then in the same way, the mandala of water dissolves outward into the subtler mandala of fire. Then, the mandala of fire dissolves outward into the even subtler mandala of wind, which finally dissolves outward into the utterly subtle mandala of space. At that point, you simply allow your mind to rest in the absence of focus of any kind but without distraction.

At this point the text mentions that, when you do these practices, and in particular the last mentioned one, as a result of working with your mind in these ways you may start seeing things or hearing things. If you do, understand such experiences to be simply a result of working with your mind and beyond that as having no significance one way or another. Do not regard them as a sign of anything special in a good way or a sign of anything special in a bad way. It does not mean that you are attaining anything in particular, but it also does not mean that you have done something wrong; it cannot hurt you. This is mentioned, because, when we have a new experience and especially when practicing meditation, we tend to react in one of two ways: we either value the experience and, therefore, naturally crave its repetition, or we fear the experience and want to be rid of it. It is important, therefore, to understand that seeing or hearing these things is in itself neither good nor bad. It has no more value or significance than a dream or any other kind of hallucination. You will not have great visions or receive prophecies because of these experiences, nor can these things you see and hear hurt you in any way.

So far, two methods of grasping the mind have been presented: grasping the mind with a conceptual focus and grasping the mind without conceptual focus. Now a third is presented, which is grasping the mind using the breathing. Here what is intended by breathing is the specific way of breathing, called vase breathing. It is called vase breathing because you use a part of your body to hold or contain the breath the way a vase contains something. However, you should be aware that there are two quite different practices called vase breathing, and the differences between them are significant. There is the vase breathing practice associated with *chandali* or *tumo* meditation and there is the vase breathing practice associated with the mahamudra tranquility meditation. Here we are concerned only with the latter. They are quite different. When you practice vase breathing as part of the *chandali* or *tumo* practice, because your intention in that practice is to generate physical heat and bliss, the vase breathing needs to be quite intense and energetic. Here, you are simply using vase breathing as a way to grasp your mind. So therefore, it is much more relaxed. The physical posture, as well, does not need to be as strict or as tense as in the *chandali* practice. You maintain the proper meditation posture of the seven dharmas of Vairochana, but beyond that there is no additional tightening up or tensing of the body.

The first thing you do when you practice vase breathing is called the cleansing or removal of stale air. Again, this is done differently depending upon what type of vase breathing you are about to practice. Here what is presented is how to cleanse or remove the stale air at the beginning of a session of mahamudra-style vase breathing. When you do it for the *chandali* or *tumo* practice, you have to do lots of stuff with your arms and hands. Here you will not be required to do that. You simply first block off or close your right nostril and then breathe out. Try to breathe out completely through your left nostril once very gently. Then you breathe out a second time, again just through the left nostril, but this time more forcefully. Then you breathe out a third and last time through the left nostril, very forcefully, completely emptying out your lungs. Then you block or close your left nostril and do exactly the same thing. You breathe out through the right nostril very gently, and then with a medium intensity, and then completely emptying your lungs. Then you rest both your hands on top of your knees and you do it a third time, but this time through both nostrils at once. So there are nine breaths that are expelled in sets of three, each set consisting of a gentle exhalation, a medium exhalation, and a forceful or vigorous exhalation.

The significance of this exercise is the same as that found in the iconography of the many deities who have three faces. Many deities have, for example, a blue central face, a white right face, and a red left face, representing what in the impure state is experienced as the three principal kleshas or mental afflictions.[12] Here, because of their correspondence to a place and therefore to nostrils and breathing, you are cleansing or removing these mental afflictions by using the breathing to do so. So as you perform these exhalations the first three times—having closed the right nostril and breathing out three times through the left nostril—you simply think that you are breathing out and removing from your system all attachment. Then, as you breathe out three times on the right side—having closed the left nostril—you simply think that you are breathing out and removing from your system all aversion. And then finally, when you breathe out three times through both nostrils at once, you think that you are breathing out or removing from your system all apathy and bewilderment.

Now, the reason why the first of each of these three sets of out breaths is gentle, the second medium, and the third forceful is that, when you breathe out the first time through your left nostril—using the first of the three sets as an example—you think that through breathing out gently you are clearing out the coarsest and, therefore, most easily removed attachment. When you breathe out a second time more forcefully, you think that as you are breathing out with medium force you are removing medium level attachment. And then finally, when you breathe out through your left nostril very forcefully, you think that you are clearing out or removing from your system the subtlest and, therefore, most difficult to remove attachment. In general, in buddhadharma, it is taught that a coarse klesha requires only a weak or gentle remedy. A klesha of middling strength that is more deeply entrenched than a coarse klesha requires a stronger remedy, while the subtlest and most deeply entrenched klesha will require the strongest remedy. In fact, you only eradicate the subtlest kleshas when you achieve the vajra-like samadhi,[13] which is the strongest remedial force. That notwithstanding, here, when you do this preparation for the practice of vase breathing, as you do the breaths you think that the corresponding kleshas have been cleared out of your system.

After removing the stale air in this way, you begin the main practice of vase breathing, which is to hold the breath. Now, there are different ways this can be done. There is what is called upper vase breath, which is holding the breath in the chest, and lower vase breath, which is holding the breath in the abdomen or belly. There is also holding the breath outside and holding the breath inside. Here, it is holding the breath inside, not outside, and it is holding the breath as a lower vase breath in the belly or abdomen, not as an upper vase breath in the chest. So all you have to do is to inhale quite slowly and gently and then, after you have inhaled, simply retain the breath that you have inhaled in your belly.

When the vase breathing practice is done in the context of *chandali,* and therefore done in a forceful manner, there are lots of additional things you have to do. For example, you have to contract the Kegel muscle to bring the lower breath up, and you have to force the breath that is brought in down, and so on.[14] Here you do not have to do any of that. Do not worry about bringing lower air up or forcing upper air down. Simply hold the air for a comfortable period in your belly, and, while holding the air, simply rest your mind in a natural and gentle way on the feeling of clear empty space that is associated with holding the breath. Remember, you are holding the breath simply in order to hold your mind; therefore, do not use any force or make any attempt to prolong the periods of breath retention. As soon as you feel uncomfortable, breathe out gently, and then breathe in again, also gently.

After doing this vase breathing several times in a session, you may practice the second part of this technique of resting the mind on the breathing, which is called resting the mind on inhalation, retention, and exhalation. Usually when we breathe, we breathe in and, as soon as we have finished breathing in, we immediately start breathing out. And as soon as we have finished breathing out, we start breathing in again. There is never any space or gap in between the in-breath and the out-breath. Now, many different ways of focusing the mind on the breathing have been taught. For example, in the hinayana abhidharma there are counting the breath, consideration of the breath, analysis of the breath, following the breath, resting the mind on the breath, and so forth. There are basically six methods taught in the abhidharma. But here we have something different from any of those. This is called gentle threefold breathing. It is called gentle because there is no particular attempt to manipulate the breathing, except that instead of breathing in and then immediately breathing out, after breathing in, you wait before you breathe out. Now this is different from the vase breathing in that here the duration of the inhalation, of the retention, and of the exhalation should all be equal, three equal periods within each complete breath.

In doing this, some people combine the phases of the breath with the mental repetition of the three mantra syllables: OM AH HUM (HUNG)— OM coordinated with the in-breath, AH with the retention of the breath, and HUM (HUNG) with the out-breath. But what is most important here is simply to recollect, as they occur, the inhalation, retention, and exhalation, so that, while you are inhaling, you are aware that you are doing so; while you are retaining the breath, you are aware that you are doing so; and while you are exhaling, you are aware that you are doing so. In the beginning, it is recommended that beginners start with doing, for example, twenty-one of these breaths as a series, and it is important to practice with enough mindfulness so that, while you breathe in, and so forth, you maintain an awareness of what part of the breathing process you are in.

So those two techniques, the vase breathing and the threefold gentle breathing, make up what is called holding or grasping the mind through breathing.

The purpose of all three of these groups of techniques—grasping the mind with a focus, grasping the mind without focus, and grasping the mind through the breathing—is to develop a state in which the mind comes naturally to rest. But this state of natural rest needs to be free of torpor and dullness. Natural rest here does not mean a state of mental vacuity, a state of mental dullness, the absence of perception or awareness. After all, the basis of the practice of meditation is the cultivation of mindfulness and alertness. Therefore, in our text and in many other texts of guidance in meditation, words like limpid clarity, glaring brilliance, and so on, are used. The use of these words indicates that, as much as the mind's coming to rest is the goal of tranquility meditation, that rest must never become a state of dullness or a state of mental vacuity or darkness. As you will see later, when you read through and study this book, it talks about this a great deal. One of its clearest statements on this subject is that the ideal state of tranquility is one in which the mind becomes as restful or calm as an ocean or lake without waves. But it goes on to say, "I do not mean a lake at night; I mean a lake during the day." By this the author is saying that if you cultivate a state of stillness in which there is no mental clarity, no lucidity, in which the mind's natural capacity for lucidity and cognition has been suppressed through the eradication of thought, there will be no benefit, even if [such a dull state of tranquility] is continued diligently for a long time.

What is needed is a state of tranquility like a calm lake or ocean during the daytime, in which the stillness of the mind is conjoined with or accompanied by a vigorous force of alertness. This means that some effort has to be placed in fostering and nurturing mindfulness and alertness. The relaxation of mind cannot be allowed to diminish the force or vigor of your alertness, because, if the mind remains vigorously alert in this way, it will be capable of applying itself to further practice; but if it becomes devoid of vigorous awareness, it will not.

To return to our outline, you will remember that the presentation of tranquility meditation in our text is divided into the general technique or general point and the specific techniques or specific methods. You will remember further that the specific methods were divided into grasping the mind when it has not been grasped, stabilizing it once it has been grasped, and progressing when it has been stabilized. So today we have completed the general technique and the first of the three sections of specific techniques. I am, therefore, going to stop with the instruction for today, and, as it seems to be pleasing to many of you, I will now meditate with you for a few minutes.

[Thrangu Rinpoche and students dedicate the merit.]

3 STABILIZING THE MIND AFTER IT HAS BEEN GRASPED

YESTERDAY, of the two main topics of our text, tranquility and insight, we began to study tranquility, and of the three sections of the presentation of tranquility meditation, we went through the first, which is grasping the mind when it is ungrasped. Today we are going to study the second section, which is stabilizing the mind after it has been grasped. This refers to the stage that comes after you have been practicing tranquility meditation and have been working with your mind for some time, and know, therefore, the basic method. You understand and have experienced the process of tranquility and can rest your mind in a state of tranquility to some degree. At this point, in order to help you progress further, the first thing that is presented is the mahabrahma samadhi of stability. Now normally, when we say mahabrahma, it refers to a god or deva of some kind. Here the term brahma is used to mean purity. So mahabrahma samadhi refers to a samadhi in which your mind's faculties, having been brought to stability, are heightened and, therefore, experienced in their purity.

The basis of this samadhi is the following visualization. In the center of your body, at the level of the heart, you visualize a four-petaled white lotus, and resting on the center of that lotus flower, you visualize a small sphere of extremely bright white light. It should be no larger than the size of a pea, and it should be visualized as very bright, even brilliant. Now, previously, in the context of grasping the mind through the breathing, you learned how to hold your breath. Here you also hold your breath. Through holding your breath, you think that you cause this tiny brilliant sphere of white light to rise up from the lotus in your heart, upward through your body, from which it emerges, shooting up out of the aperture at the center of the top of your head, and continues to rise until it reaches the highest reaches of space above you. While doing this, you also put more exertion into your physical posture, so that your posture is especially strict, involving even a little tension. You also raise your gaze, so that you are looking upward, and attempt to make your mind very bright, clear, and cheerful.

This meditation is useful if you find that your mind is unclear, torpid or depressed, or when you find yourself uninterested in practice and your mind dull. The mahabrahma samadhi of stability will serve to cheer you up and to clarify, or promote lucidity in, your mind. In the practice of both tranquility and insight, torpor is a problem. But it is especially a problem for practitioners of tranquility, because the practice of tranquility meditation, by its very nature, emphasizes the achievement of stillness, and stillness can, if you are not attentive, produce a state of torpor. This technique is introduced at this point to enable one to maintain stillness while dispelling the torpor that can accompany it. For the proper practice of tranquility meditation, the mind's lucidity needs to be at full strength. It should not be weakened in anyway by the stillness one is cultivating. So this practice helps within the context of stillness to promote and even increase the mind's lucidity.

The second meditation in this section of tranquility instruction is called the subterranean samadhi, which is similar in a way to the previous instruction, except that it is a remedy for exactly the opposite problem. Sometimes we find that our minds are unable to come to rest, that we are excited by the thoughts that pass through our minds and cannot let go of them. Generally, this is some kind of pleasant excitement during which you cannot stop yourself from recollecting pleasant things, pleasant memories, and so on. It is like, for example, when you are so excited by something that you cannot go to sleep. This obviously disturbs the practice of meditation.

A second, and in some ways similar state, is one in which you are disturbed by thoughts of intense regret, regretting things you have done or things that have happened in the past that you cannot let go of. In either case, whether it is excitement or regret, it is equally disturbing to the practice of meditation, because it causes the mind to become unstable. This meditation—the subterranean samadhi—is designed to serve as a remedy or antidote for this problem. Here in the center of your body, at the level of the heart, you visualize a lotus flower as before, except that here, because you are visualizing the flower in order to pacify or cool down the mind, instead of visualizing it as white, you visualize it as black. Also, because you are trying to bring your mind's energy downward, you visualize the lotus flower as facing downward. And then you think that resting on the center of the lotus flower which is facing downward—and, of course, now on the underside— is a tiny sphere of black light, again visualized as no larger than a pea, so that the meditation is sharply focused. Then you think that the sphere of black light descends from where it starts out, down through your body, comes out the bottom, and continues going down very far into and below the ground. Furthermore, while doing this, you think that this sphere of black light is not something physically light, but very heavy, and that its heaviness or weight causes it to descend through and below the earth.

At this point, two techniques have been presented in this section. The first, the mahabrahma samadhi, is presented as a remedy for dullness, and the second, the subterranean samadhi, as a remedy for the wildness of either excitement or regret. The third instruction presented here is simply to apply either one of these as needed, depending upon your experience. Any given person will at different times experience both torpor and wildness of mind. So when your mind is dull, you practice the mahabhrama samadhi, and when your mind is wild, you practice the subterranean samadhi. That you should apply these two meditations as needed constitutes the third instruction in this section.

Many problems can come up in the practice of meditation. By problems here I do not mean final impediments that will destroy the path, but temporary stumbling blocks. Of these, two are the most common: torpor and wildness of mind. These techniques are presented here in order to overcome these two tendencies. You pacify the tendency to torpor by practicing the mahabhrama samadhi; you pacify the tendency to wildness and excitement by practicing the subterranean samadhi. It is necessary to overcome both of these tendencies so that your mind can come to rest naturally.

Next, in the second of the three sections that make up the presentation of tranquility meditation, comes the instruction in the nine methods or stages of bringing the mind to rest. The first of the nine is called placement. Placement here simply means the initial process of bringing the mind to some kind of rest or stability. This is accomplished by applying the methods taught under the category of grasping the mind when it is ungrasped. As you will remember, this process consists of training the sixth consciousness not to follow or be caught by the thoughts that arise within it. These thoughts are of various kinds, but regardless of the thought's content, it is to be treated in the same way at this stage. Thoughts can be very negative, they can be made up of various kleshas, they can be what we regard as unvirtuous, but one does not follow them in the practice of tranquility. And even if thoughts are virtuous, in the practice of tranquility meditation they are still regarded as a potential source of disturbance. Usually we think that virtuous thoughts are not a problem, but in the practice of tranquility meditation a virtuous thought can be just as disturbing or distracting as an unvirtuous one. So therefore, in this first of the nine stages or nine methods of bringing the mind to rest, you are attempting to maintain a state in which your mind is placed at rest, and yet without impairing the mind's lucidity. The mind is still and at rest, but not dull, and maintains its brilliant lucidity. Now, at this stage, which is the stage of a beginning practitioner of tranquility meditation, this state will not last very long. Nevertheless, getting your mind to the point at which it comes to rest while maintaining its natural lucidity, for however brief a period, is the first of the nine stages—placement.

When you practice this first discipline, the discipline of placement, repeatedly, eventually there occurs some prolonging of the state of stillness, the state of the mind being at rest. This state of rest, which was previously achieved as the first of the nine stages, when somewhat prolonged, constitutes the second stage, called prolonged placement. It is the same state of rest as experienced in the first stage, but here it is lasting longer.

Then, through cultivating the second stage, you reach the third stage, which has two different names. In this text it is called definite placement or certain placement, but in other contexts it is called returning placement. While returning placement is not the term used in this text, it is perhaps the most descriptive term for this stage, and for the following reason. In achieving the third stage you are obviously still practicing the second, which means that you are working with a somewhat prolonged state of stillness. Nevertheless, it is not prolonged indefinitely. At some point thoughts arise. The discipline and practice of the third stage consists of not wandering on the basis of the arising of a thought, not being caught by it, not following it, but instead, recognizing that a thought has arisen. When a thought arises, one recognizes it, thinking, "A thought has arisen; my mind is not at rest," and on the basis of that recognition, one returns to the state of stillness. That is why the most descriptive term for the third stage is returning placement, although in our text it is called certain or definite placement.

The fourth method of resting the mind, called close placement, refers to resting in the state of stillness to which you have returned when, through applying the mindfulness and alertness enjoined in the third method, you have recognized the arising of a thought and have been able to return to that state of placement or stillness. So, close placement consists of resting in or remaining in placement subsequent to your return to that state. But despite such resting, there will continue to be disturbances of various kinds. Sometimes you might be disturbed by your thoughts; sometimes your mind might become dull or torpid or sleepy; sometimes you may be afflicted by lack of interest in the practice itself. The next two methods, the fifth and the sixth, are both remedies to these problems. Either one can be applied as a remedy. However, they are enumerated separately because they are different techniques or methods.

The fifth, which is called taming, is recollection of the qualities or benefits of samadhi. When your mind is torpid or disturbed, when it is difficult to practice, when you find yourself uninterested in practice, the fifth method, taming, is a way of recollecting why you are practicing tranquility meditation and the benefits of doing so. The immediate benefits of tranquility meditation are physical and mental well-being. The ultimate benefit of tranquility meditation is the pacification of kleshas or mental afflictions. Now, we cannot say the eradication of mental afflictions, because tranquility alone is insufficient to eradicate mental afflictions. That is accomplished through insight meditation. The reason tranquility alone cannot eradicate the afflictions is that it does not contain enough discernment, enough prajna. But tranquility does weaken the mental afflictions. Literally the Tibetan term used here, *gö nönpa*, means "to suppress," but it is not suppression in the sense of repression of mental afflictions, it is more the idea of debilitating or weakening the mental afflictions. In any case, through the application of the fifth method you promote your enthusiasm for the practice by recollecting its benefits, and to the degree one generates enthusiasm, one's enthusiasm naturally and spontaneously reduces the amount of effort required to bring the mind to rest. The more enthusiastic you are about the practice, the more effortlessly your mind will come to rest.

For example, in the life of Jetsun Milarepa, soon after he had received his initial instruction from Lord Marpa, he went into retreat in a cave called Tiger Nak at the Southern Cliffs, near Marpa's residence. While Milarepa was in retreat there, Marpa came to see him and said to Milarepa, "You are practicing very diligently, but why do you not take a break?"

And Milarepa said, "I do not need to take a break; practice itself is taking a break."

Milarepa perceived practice as a state of rest or a state of relaxation because of his enthusiasm for it. Because he was so enthusiastic, he perceived diligent practice as effortless. Now, we are not Milarepa, but nevertheless, to the extent that we recollect the benefits of tranquility meditation, to the same extent we will perceive it as effortless.

The sixth method of resting the mind deals in some cases with the same problems and in other cases with similar problems as dealt with by the fifth. In the fifth, the mind is tamed or subdued through the recollection of the benefits of the samadhi of stillness. In the sixth, called pacification, the mind is pacified through recollecting what is wrong with thoughts. Often, when we are overpowered by our thoughts—when we cannot stop thinking—it is because we regard the particular thoughts that we are entertaining as either valuable because they are pleasurable or valuable because they are in some way important. In either case, the problem is that we are attaching some kind of undeserved value and importance to the thoughts. That is why we hold onto them. The sixth method is simply to recollect that in the context of meditation practice, thoughts are completely useless. They serve no function. They are no good whatsoever. They are a complete waste of time. And they impede the practice of dharma. This recollection of what is wrong with thinking will naturally cause you to stop liking thoughts, and when you do not like them, when you do not enjoy thinking, then you will not need to repress your thoughts; you will not need to try consciously to stop thinking, because if you do not like something, you simply will not do it. So the sixth method, called pacification, is to recollect the defects of thinking.

The seventh method of resting the mind is called thorough pacification. Now, sometimes when we practice meditation, there are no problems, and as long as there are no problems, as long as your mind is not distracted or disturbed, you simply continue in the state of placement. But sometimes, of course, there are problems, and here the point is not to attempt to solve these problems—specifically the disturbances caused by thoughts—through force. One is not to attempt to force thoughts not to arise by thinking, "I must not allow my mind to move at all." Here the method employed involves selecting one thought, or one type of thought, from among the many that might be arising in your mind and rest in that. Thoughts can arise with unlimited variety of content. We have all kinds of thoughts. Especially disturbing thoughts include thoughts of spite, the wish to harm someone, thoughts of jealousy or competitiveness, and thoughts of regret and guilt. Pleasant thoughts include thoughts of excitement, recollection of pleasure, and so forth. In this method you recognize one particular thought that has arisen— and here you are not treating thought as an abstraction or a generality, but you are working with one particular thought—and you rest in that thought. When you rest in that thought, you are not attempting to fight the thought. You are not attempting to get rid of it, stop it or suppress it. You are resting in it, and when you rest in it, the thought dissolves. Now in the text it says that, if through resting in a thought you succeed in thoroughly recognizing its nature, the stuff of which it is made, it will be self-liberated. This method of resting in the thought rather than attempting to suppress it is the seventh technique, thorough pacification.

Through the application of the first seven methods of resting the mind, you achieve the ability to apply the eighth and ninth methods. The eighth is called unification. Unification here refers to the stage at which, through the preceding diligent application of the fifth, sixth, and seventh methods as remedies for problems in meditation, you no longer need to apply force in your meditation practice. You are no longer trying to force anything. Therefore, there is no fluctuation or oscillation between the state of relaxed meditation and the state of forced meditation in response to problems. So the eighth method or stage, unification, really refers to the point when your mind is resting naturally.

This in turn leads to the ninth and last stage, called even placement, which is a state in which there is no longer any distraction. The term even or equal here means specifically that your mind is in a state of placement free both of the defects of tension and of excessive, sloppy relaxation. The absence of tension and of the need for force, and the absence of sloppy relaxation or distraction allow the quality of the placement of your mind, of the resting of your mind, to become thoroughly even or equal.

These nine methods of resting the mind are presented so that you understand what tranquility meditation is, what the process of bringing the mind to stillness is, and how to proceed or get on with it. Therefore, the presentation of these two topics—the nine methods of resting the mind and the preceding three samadhis practiced as remedies or antidotes for disturbances—make up the second of the three sections here, which is stabilizing the mind after it has been gotten hold of or grasped.

So at this point we have completed the first two of the three sections of the presentation of tranquility meditation—grasping the mind when it is ungrasped and stabilizing it when it has been grasped—and each contains various sections. If you look at your text you will see that these subsections are numbered as teaching sessions and as practice sessions. These are two parallel numbering systems that are nevertheless different from each other.

If you have any questions at this point about what we have discussed so far, please feel free to ask them.

Question: I have questions concerning Tibetan terminology and its translation. First, what is really meant by thought or *namtok*. Discursive thought is one type of *namtok*. Then there is a kind of visual thought that is on the surface of the mind, like daydreaming, for example, when you are thinking about going somewhere. Daydreamy thoughts seem to be very much on the surface of the mind and usually move slowly. Then there is what we call *klesha*. Is *klesha* included in *namtok*? And then there is a kind of visual thought that one becomes aware of, and my suspicion is that this is part of the *okju* or undercurrent of subtle thoughts, but I'm not sure. This type of thought is visual, though it moves through the mind very, very fast, much too fast to daydream about or speculate about; in fact, it usually moves so fast one cannot even recognize the images as they go though; it is just going through like a high speed train. Again, I suspect that this falls in the category of subtle thought. And then I'm wondering if there is similar subtle discursive thought.

By discursive thought I mean that kind of thought that is made up of words, as when you are talking to yourself. So when you are saying, "thought," I'm wondering if you could be very precise as to what kind of thought you are referring, whether visual thought or discursive, linguistic, verbal thought. And as to these two types of thoughts, do they both occur as coarse thoughts and as subtle thoughts in the undercurrent of thought?

Rinpoche: Well! [laughter] In brief—yes [more laughter]. The answer to this question is found in *pramana,* the study of valid cognition. There a division of thoughts into images and linguistic thoughts is mentioned. The thoughts that you were describing as visual images are called abstractions. Now, normally we use the word abstraction to mean a linguistic concept of something, but here mental visual images are called abstractions or generalizations because they constitute the sixth consciousness' replication or replica of sensory information, in the example you gave, of visual images of an eye consciousness.[15] So the type of thought that you are describing is categorized as a generalization based on sense information, and in spite of the term *dönchi* or generalization or abstraction, it is still primarily visual rather than linguistic. It is characterized as a thought and can either have a coarse obvious presence or be a part of the undercurrent of subtle thought.

The second type of thought that you are describing, which is for humans linguistic thought, is said in the literature of valid cognition to have two divisions or two sub-varieties. One is thoughts which are based upon the apprehension of a thing and the linguistic concept of that thing as being inherently connected or as being the same. That is something that humans have because we have language. The other variety of this is called the possibility of confusing a thing and a concept or association with that thing. So to be clear and to be brief the difference between these two is that one is a fully developed linguistic thought and the other is a process of mental association. The latter, the thoughts of association, are found more in animals and in human infants. For example, an animal will not have a linguistic concept for water. It does not think water or have any other linguistic concept for it. However, when it hears water but cannot see it, the animal will have a reaction to that sound through association, and that is the equivalent in an animal of a linguistic concept, according to the study of valid cognition. This is also very prevalent among humans in early infancy.

Among older humans what takes the place of this association is much more linguistically oriented. Most of the linguistic thinking that we do is based upon the full association or full mixing up of a thing and the linguistic concept we use to designate it. Another term for this is the confusion of appearance for its designation, or you could say it the other way around, the confusion of the designation for its appearance. For example, when we use the word water to refer to water, there is no inherent reason why the sound of that particular word should mean that particular thing. Nevertheless, once we have absorbed or imbibed that linguistic concept, we think of them as the same, which they are not. So this type of thought, linguistic thought, can also be both coarse and subtle. It can be fully manifested in the mind or it can be present as part of the undercurrent as well.

Now about the term *namtok* (in Tibetan) or *vikulpa* (in Sanskrit), the term *tokpa,* which also means thought, simply refers to a mental event that constitutes some kind of upsurge of the mind's capacity to conceptualize. The adjective *nampar* or *vi* in *vikulpa,* which means complete, means that the thought is fully developed. Nevertheless, even the undercurrent, as subtle as it is, is still considered to be *vikulpa* or *namtok*—fully developed thought—and does not have to be called only *tokpa.*

Question: So if you catch it at the upsurge, does that mean *namtok* does not arise?

Rinpoche: Well basically *tokpa* is understood as a cognitive event and *namtok* means a prominent upsurge of that, and that is why the word for realization is linguistically related to *tokpa*; it is almost the same, because of the basic idea that *tokpa* refers to cognition or knowing primarily, and *namtok* to a full-blown conceptuality.

Question: What is the difference between the self-liberation in the seventh stage and the self-liberation in the mahamudra tradition?

Rinpoche: As you mentioned in your question, the term self-liberation is used in both cases, but it has somewhat different meanings. In the case of the seventh of the nine methods of resting the mind, it refers to the fact that without one's having to get rid of the thought, it simply dissolves naturally of itself. In the context of mahamudra, self-liberation refers to the irrelevance of thought because there is recognition of the mind's nature.[16]

We have to stop here.

[Thrangu Rinpoche and students dedicate the merit.]

4 Bringing Progress to the Mind That Has Been Stabilized

IN *The Ocean of Definitive Meaning,* the instructions on tranquility meditation are divided into three sections: grasping the mind that has not yet
been grasped; stabilizing the mind after it has been grasped; and bringing
progress to the mind that has been stabilized. These three sections are presented because they are necessary as three stages of instruction when one
actually practices. The first section is designed to teach someone who does
not yet know how to rest their mind how to do so. But that in itself is not
enough. Because once one knows how to rest the mind, one needs actually
to achieve stability in doing so. For that reason the second section is taught.
Now, during the two sessions on the first day I presented the instruction of
the first section and yesterday morning those of the second. This morning we
are going to go on to the third section, which concerns making progress after
stabilization has been achieved. This third set of instructions is needed
because, even though you know how to bring the mind to rest and you
understand how to make that state of rest or stillness stable, you need further
to know how to enhance it or cause it to develop.

The first two sections or stages of tranquility instruction were largely concerned with meditation and not much with post-meditation. The third section of instruction, enhancement or progress, is concerned equally with
meditation and post-meditation. These instructions teach us how to remain
undistracted from the state of tranquility or stillness not only during meditation but in post-meditation as well, because it is only by maintaining con-
tinuously this state free of distraction that progress or enhancement can
occur.

Whether we are meditating or in post-meditation, we continue physically
to see, which means that our eyes continue to contact the physical forms
that are their sense objects. We continue to hear sounds, and thoughts continue to arise. These forms that we see with our eyes we tend to appraise in
various ways. Some we designate as good, others as bad, and so on. When we
lack instruction, we are distracted by the forms that we see. Our minds fol-

low the eye consciousness because we have no faculty of mindfulness and no faculty of alertness[17] to prevent the mind from following the eye consciousness. The second section of tranquility instruction, which we studied yesterday—stabilizing the mind that has been grasped—was essentially concerned with the cultivation of the dual faculties of mindfulness and alertness. So now, in the third section, you are going to learn how to apply these faculties that have been cultivated, not only in meditation but in post-meditation as well, and with reference to the experience of forms and sounds and so forth.

Here it is taught that when you see a form, you continue to maintain mindfulness and alertness while seeing it, so that your mind does not run wild on the basis of having seen it. Normally, when we lack instruction, our minds are unattended. Unattended means that we allow them to run wild. The remedy for this tendency of the unattended mind to run wild is to attend it through the application of mindfulness and alertness. There is a specific form of these which is called "watchfulness." The term watchfulness has been used by the siddhas of our lineage to mean a way of being aware of what the mind is doing that is something like the activity of a spy who is following someone and observes everything that they do and everywhere they go. Throughout the day, from the morning until we go to sleep, our minds continue to move. They respond to forms that are seen, sounds that are heard, and thoughts that arise. Lacking mindfulness and alertness, lacking the presence of watchfulness, we are usually unaware of the details. Distracted by forms and sounds, we become unaware of the details of the forms and sounds themselves; everything becomes very vague because of the distraction. This distraction is the mind's being allowed to drift aimlessly, and in fact the word that we use for distraction, for a state of full distraction, literally means fully drifting. The drifting here is said to be like the drifting of a piece of driftwood on the surface of an ocean. In response to the currents and waves in the water, it goes all over the place. In the same way, when the mind is unattended by watchfulness, your mind just drifts without any direction whatsoever. So, in order to impose watchfulness on this situation, the first technique taught here is using the faculty of watchfulness in connection with seeing visual form.

As I mentioned yesterday, the sense consciousnesses, such as the eye consciousness, are not conceptual consciousnesses. So, for example, the eye consciousness sees everything that it sees, but whether what it sees is what we would regard as good or what we would regard as bad, the eye consciousness itself makes no such appraisal. It does not appraise or consider what it sees; it simply sees. Therefore, the sense consciousnesses, such as the eye consciousness, cannot perform the act or functions of mindfulness and alertness. It is the sixth consciousness that follows the sense consciousnesses, that considers and appraises what is experienced by the sense consciousnesses; and it is the sixth consciousness that must be brought to perform the functions of mindfulness and alertness. This is true of the sixth consciousness in relation to all the five senses. We see forms and then these forms are perceived by the sixth consciousness as pleasant or unpleasant. Sounds, which are initially experienced by the ear consciousness, are perceived by the sixth consciousness as pleasant sounds or unpleasant. Tastes are perceived by the sixth consciousness as bitter or sweet; smells by the sixth consciousness as fragrant or repulsive; and tactile sensations by the sixth consciousness as pleasurable or unpleasurable. When the sixth consciousness follows any of the five sense consciousnesses without the presence of mindfulness and alertness, when it is allowed simply to drift, then we are, if I may use a negative analogy, almost like walking corpses, because there is no mindfulness or alertness; there is no presence or conscious presence within what we are experiencing. Therefore, it has been said by the yogis of the past, "Just as your body should remain on its seat, your mind should remain in your body."

Now, in order to be mindful, your mind, which functions through the senses, and, therefore, is connected with your body, has to be consciously present within your body. You must be present in and aware of what you are experiencing through the senses. You are always seeing and hearing and so on, but what is being said here is that you must be consciously aware of what you are seeing, consciously aware of what you are hearing, and so on. This does not mean that you attempt to interfere with or in any way stop, limit, or block what you see or what you hear. It means simply that you must know what you are seeing, know what you are hearing, and so on. This practice of presence and awareness will greatly help the practice of meditation.

All of that is with reference to the sixth consciousness' functioning on the basis of and following on the experiences of the five sense consciousnesses. But the sixth consciousness also has activities that are internal to itself, which is to say, the arising of thoughts which are not necessarily directly caused by something appearing to the five sense consciousnesses. Now, different sorts of thoughts arise in our minds. Sometimes we have thoughts that traditionally we think of as ones we should reject, unvirtuous thoughts, defined here as thoughts arising out of mental afflictions or kleshas, such as attachment, aversion, and so on. Then sometimes we have thoughts that we would normally identify as virtuous, thoughts we wish to encourage and undertake. And then sometimes we have thoughts that are neutral and that we regard in that way as irrelevant. Here you are not attempting to limit what type of thoughts arise in your mind; you are simply attempting to recognize what thoughts arise in your mind. In the context of tranquility meditation, it means to recognize them as what they are in terms of their content. So, if virtuous thoughts arise in your mind, recognize them as virtuous; if negative thoughts arise, recognize them as negative; if neutral thoughts arise, recognize them as neutral. You are simply trying to maintain the awareness of recognizing what is happening in your mind. This is different from recognizing the nature of thought, which will be taught later when we come to the practice of insight meditation. Here you are not attempting to see the nature of thought, but simply to recognize the presence or appearance of thoughts within your mind. And this is to be attempted not only when you are meditating but also in post-meditation, when you are busy—when you are eating or walking or working or talking and so on.

Now, in spite of the fact that you are to be aware of what type of thoughts arise in this phase of the practice, it is not recommended that you view thoughts as an enemy. You are not attempting to stop them from arising, you are simply not allowing yourself to drift in following thoughts.[18] The practice here is simply to be aware of the thoughts that arise in your mind.

Furthermore, it says in our text that this awareness should be relaxed. The amount of effort engaged in this awareness should be just enough so that the thread or continuity of the awareness does not break. Through developing and maintaining this type of awareness there will occur progress in your meditation.

In the songs of practitioners of the past it says, "Do not see thoughts as something you have to get rid of, and do not see the absence of thoughts as something you have to acquire; just cultivate watchfulness, and genuine tranquility will arise." In trying to develop watchfulness, you are not attempting to stop thinking but simply to be aware of what arises in the mind.

Now, for ordinary individuals this watchfulness is not going to be constant in the beginning. Initially it will be sporadic. On the other hand, this watchfulness is not utterly beyond us. It can be cultivated if we put in the necessary effort. The function of watchfulness is that it will enable you not to be disturbed; it will enable your meditation not to be harmed by the necessary actions you engage in throughout the day. And that absence of disturbance or distraction will bring enhancement and progress to your practice of meditation.

Here two methods are presented that, according to the teachings, need to be practiced or cultivated in order to develop the right degree of effort in the cultivation of mindfulness and alertness. These methods are tension and relaxation. It is taught that they need to be practiced in alternation so that you can experience the right balance between them in the practice of mindfulness. In order to practice tension, sometimes you intentionally tighten your awareness—focus your awareness as sharply and as vigorously as you can—in the practice of mindfulness. In order to do so, you actually even tighten up your body, including your physical muscles. You generate the intention, "I will not allow the slightest distraction to occur," and with that motivating force, you tighten up your mind and your body, even up to your mouth and your nose, and be as tight as you can in not allowing distraction.

Then when you practice relaxation, you consciously let go of all tension, relax all tension. The watchfulness you practice in that way is like watching someone or something from a distance.

Now, in tension you are learning to cultivate the vigor of awareness, and in relaxation you are learning to cultivate the relaxed and steady quality of awareness. In relaxation you are not really letting go of the faculty of watchfulness itself, but simply of unnecessary effort. So, practicing these two in alternation will teach you how to cultivate watchfulness.

In each major section, *The Ocean of Definitive Meaning* is divided concurrently in two different ways—into teaching sessions and practice sessions. A teaching session will contain something you need to know about that stage of the practice, and a practice session will contain instruction for that specific stage of mahamudra practice. For example, in this section, the last section of tranquility instruction, there is only one practice session, which means that it is taught as one unified practice, the cultivation of the watchfulness of mindfulness and alertness. This watchfulness is to be applied to whatever you experience: to visible forms, audible sounds, thoughts, and so on. All of this is presented as one unit, as one practice. On the other hand, so that this practice of watchfulness and its implications are clearly understood, in this same section there are also three teaching sessions.

In the second of the teaching sessions we find twelve questions about the practice of tranquility meditation and about the experience of it. If you read these in your book, you will find that the questions are presented together with their answers, and that they will help to dispel any doubts or confusion you may have about the experience of tranquility meditation.

Among these questions the most important concerns a phenomenon that can occur in meditation practice that here is called "rainbow meditation." Rainbow meditation refers to the intentional cultivation of a beautiful, pleasant meditative state that is utterly useless. Rainbows are very pretty; they have nice colors and are very bright and it is nice to look at them, but they serve no function. You cannot eat them, you cannot wear them, you cannot live in them. In the same way, it sometimes happens that, when we experience some kind of well-being or pleasure in meditation, we make a goal out of it, and we attempt to fabricate or repeat that particular meditative state. The pleasure itself is like a rainbow; it is pretty, but it is useless. As is pointed out in our text, meditation is not supposed to be the fabrication or the reinforcement of some particular state, but simply the cultivation of the awareness of whatever is arising in the mind.

A second issue that is brought up in these twelve questions is the issue of no alteration. We are instructed not to alter what arises in the mind, but not altering what arises in the mind does not mean that we do not need mindfulness and alertness. We do, and it is possible to misunderstand the instruction of no alteration to mean not even engaging in the actions of mindfulness and alertness and, therefore, not even possessing watchfulness. When we misunderstand the idea of relaxation and spontaneity and no alteration, then we let our minds drift just as they did when we were not practicing meditation at all, and this is letting go in the wrong way. We need to cultivate mindfulness and alertness, so do not misunderstand no alteration, relaxation, letting go, and so forth to mean no imposition of mindfulness.

The third question concerns quite a common problem [that can occur after you have learned to meditate and even after you have had good meditation experiences.] You have received sufficient instruction, but you stop meditating. This is called abandoned or disowned meditation. Now, in the beginning the first thing we need to do, of course, is to learn how to meditate. This is taught primarily in the section called grasping the ungrasped mind. But once we have learned how to meditate and how to grasp the ungrasped mind, we need actually to apply these instructions, as taught here primarily in this third section, or the facility we have gained in meditation will degenerate or be lost altogether. We need to make use of the instructions we have received by applying them diligently. We need to apply watchfulness all the time. Otherwise, if you leave your meditation practice unattended or abandoned, then there is really no point in having received instructions from your teachers in the first place.

The fourth question is also very important. When we meditate, sometimes the experience of meditation will be pleasant or pleasurable, and sometimes that sensation or experience of well-being will simply not be there. It is important not to be affected by this. Whatever happens in your meditation, whether it is pleasant or not, it is important simply to continue. There is a danger of becoming used to an experience of well-being that has arisen in meditation and of craving it, and, therefore, of becoming disappointed and discouraged if it vanishes. The point here is not to be influenced by what arises in meditation, whether it be pleasurable or not, and simply to continue practicing no matter what happens.

In that way there are altogether twelve questions with their answers in this section of the book, and you should read them.

The third teaching session in this section concerns the importance of devotion, which is held to be the single most significant and effective source of progress and enhancement in meditation practice. Therefore, since devotion is so important, it is recommended that you supplement your practice from time to time with the practice of guru yoga. One could chant and do the meditations of an entire guru yoga practice and use that as a basis for devoted supplication. Through the cultivation of devotion in that way, a meditation practice that lacks lucidity will gain lucidity, that lacks stability will gain stability, and so on. So, if you have time to perform a guru yoga practice, this is very much recommended for the cultivation of devotion. If you lack the time or circumstances to do so, then you should attempt to achieve the same results through the practice of some short supplication. For example, when we recite the lineage supplication at the beginning of teaching sessions, do not do so mindlessly or by rote. Consciously recite the supplication, applying your mindfulness to its meaning, so that through it you can cultivate devotion. That completes a brief presentation of the instructions on tranquility meditation found in *The Ocean of Definitive Meaning*.

Now, in the cultivation of the path of method, three things are necessary: the empowerments which ripen, the reading transmissions which provide support, and the instructions which bring liberation. For the practice of the path of liberation, however, there is no particular empowerment that is required, because the practice itself consists of the two practices of tranquility and insight alone. Nevertheless, one does need instruction, which I am providing, and one also should receive the reading transmission for the text that is being used as the basis of instruction. Therefore, I am now going to start to give, one section at a time, the reading transmission for *The Ocean of Definitive Meaning*. While I do so, please listen attentively and especially with pure motivation.

[Rinpoche begins the reading transmission.]

[Rinpoche and students dedicate the merit.]

5 THE PRACTICE OF INSIGHT, WHICH ERADICATES THE KLESHAS

THIS MORNING we finished the section of our text that describes the practice of tranquility. Next we come to the practice of insight. We have to begin with the practice of tranquility because, although we have the innate capacity to recognize our mind's nature, this capacity is obstructed by the disturbance of thoughts. Thoughts disturb our minds; therefore, the first step in coming to a recognition of the mind's nature is to pacify the thoughts and thereby stop the disturbance.

In the *Aspiration of Mahamudra* by the Third Gyalwang Karmapa, Rangjung Dorje,[19] it says, "May the waves of coarse and subtle thoughts be pacified in their own place; may the ocean of the mind abide naturally undisturbed by the wind of distraction, free of the sediment of torpor and dullness; may the water of the mind rest in flawless tranquility." The image used here is the surface of a body of water. A body of water has the natural ability to reflect. For example, a body of water can reflect the moon and stars and so forth that are in the sky above it, but there are two things that can prevent that from happening. If the surface of the water is agitated by the wind and, therefore, has waves, it will not reflect properly. Nor will it reflect properly if the water itself is pervaded by sludge or sediment. Our minds are like that body of water, prevented from being as lucid as they naturally can be by two things: coarse and subtle thoughts, which are like the wind that causes waves on the surface of a body of water; and dullness in the mind, which is like sediment in a body of water. The latter includes all states of torpor and mental obscurity or dullness. The purpose of tranquility meditation is to pacify and, thereby, remove these two impediments—thoughts and dullness.

Tranquility meditation pacifies thought, and because thought is the medium for kleshas, it also leads to the pacification of kleshas. This in turn leads to considerable relaxation and tranquility of mind, which produces many benefits and qualities, but by itself tranquility meditation cannot eradicate the kleshas. They can be and are weakened by the practice of tranquility meditation, but they cannot be and are not eradicated by it. Only prajna can eradicate the kleshas, and there simply is not enough prajna present in the practice of tranquility meditation.

Now, of course, some prajna is generated by the practice of tranquility alone, because, when the mind comes to rest, the mind's natural lucidity is heightened. Nevertheless, this lucidity of cognition is not particularly emphasized in tranquility meditation; therefore, the full-blown prajna of meditation is not developed by the practice of tranquility alone. Tranquility meditation alone cannot eradicate the kleshas; the meditation that leads to the eradication of kleshas is insight meditation, because insight leads to the development of discernment (Sanskrit: *prajna;* Tibetan: *sherab)* and of wisdom (Sanskrit: *jnana;* Tibetan: *yeshe).*

When the Buddha Shakyamuni came into this world, he turned the wheel of dharma, which is to say, he bestowed the instructions that form the basis for our practice. The first of his three turnings of the dharma wheel is called the dharma wheel or dharmachakra of the four noble truths. The four noble truths present the basic structure of the Buddhist path and approach. They present an outline of how one can immediately set about achieving liberation. These four truths start with what we are principally concerned with, which is how to become free of suffering. Of course, we cannot become free of suffering just by trying to become free of suffering. We cannot stop suffering by itself. Instead, we first have to identify and remove the cause or causes of suffering. Thus, the first noble truth is the truth of suffering, and the second noble truth is the truth of the cause of suffering, identified as karma[20] and kleshas.[21]

The third noble truth, the truth of the cessation of suffering, explains what happens when you get rid of all karma and all kleshas. Because of the cessation of the cause of suffering—because of the absence of kleshas—the cessation of suffering comes about as a natural result. So the third noble truth presents the freedom that results from practice.

The fourth noble truth presents the method, referred to as the path, through which that freedom, that cessation from suffering, is achieved. According to the Buddha's teaching, this path is to be consciously and gradually cultivated.

These first teachings given by the Buddha form the basis of all his subsequent teachings. They are fundamental to everything he taught, and so they are appropriate for someone beginning the path. In the second and third dharmachakras he expanded on these four truths, principally by explaining in much greater detail what the path consists of and what the methods for accomplishing it are. For example, he taught the prajnaparamita sutras at Vulture Peak Mountain, near Rajagriha. These sutras exist now in longer, middling, and shorter forms. The most concise of these, and also the best known, is the *Heart Sutra*.[22] If you look at that sutra, you will see that the Buddha was teaching emptiness at that time. The reason for teaching emptiness is that, as we have seen in the outline of the four noble truths, if we want to be free of suffering, we have to abandon the cause of suffering, which is the kleshas. But just as we cannot simply abandon suffering by wanting to, we cannot simply abandon kleshas or let go of kleshas by wanting to either. The only way to actually abandon or eradicate the kleshas is to see their nature. Therefore, in order to abandon the kleshas, we must cultivate the prajna or discernment which is able to see the nature of those kleshas. If their nature is seen, they will disappear by themselves without having to be chased away or destroyed by any other means.

So in order to cultivate this prajna,[23] the Buddha taught emptiness. He taught that there is no truly existent person who generates kleshas, that there is no truly existent object that stimulates kleshas, that the kleshas themselves have no solid or substantial existence, and so forth. He taught that what we experience exists as relative truth, but that the emptiness of what we experience is absolute truth. These explanations, such as are found in the *Heart Sutra,* make up the second turning of the dharmachakra. More elaborate presentations of the same prajnaparamita teachings are found in *The Hundred Thousand Stanza Prajnaparamita Sutra, The Eight Thousand Stanza Prajnaparamita Sutra,* and so forth.

In the second dharmachakra, the Buddha taught or demonstrated that all phenomena are empty, that emptiness is the nature of all things. In the third dharmachakra, he presented in great detail what the nature of emptiness is. Therefore, the third dharmachakra is called "The Dharmachakra of Fine Distinctions," which includes sutras such as the *Lankavatara Sutra*, the *Samadhiraja Sutra,* the *Lotus Sutra,* and so forth. To assemblies of bodhisattvas and shravakas the Buddha taught in these sutras that, while it is the case, as he had previously taught, that all phenomena are empty, that emptiness, which is the single nature of all phenomena, is not nothingness. It is emptiness, but it is at the same time lucidity or clarity; it is not nothingness like space, but is rather the open expansive presence of wisdom.

Now, these teachings of the second and third dharmachakras were gradually elaborated on, explained, and propagated by great pandits and siddhas. They are summarized and embodied in some of the vajrayana teachings that we practice. You can see a summary of these teachings, for example, in the shunyata mantra, which is often used at the commencement of a generation stage practice.[24] After the preliminary syllable OM,[25] the first word in the mantra is SHUNYATA, which means emptiness. It is shunyata or emptiness that is, in the final analysis, the principal concern or principal message of both the sutras and the tantras. It is shunyata that is to be realized. However, it needs to be understood that shunyata is not nothingness; it is at the same time wisdom. Therefore, after the word shunyata, comes the word JNANA, which means wisdom. Furthermore, while this empty wisdom is the nature of all things, it is also unchanging. It is not the case that sometimes things are empty and sometimes they are not, that sometimes the nature of that emptiness is wisdom and sometimes it is not. It is utterly unchanging. Therefore, the next word is VAJRA, which in this context means that which is indestructible and unchanging. The mantra concludes with the statement, SOBAWA ATMAKO HAM, which means, "That is my nature." The message of this mantra is simply that this indestructible union of emptiness and wisdom is the nature of all beings and all things. Because this is our nature, we need to meditate on it and we need to recognize it. We need to recognize it, because it is what we truly are.

Then, how do we meditate on this nature? There are two approaches: one is to take inferential valid cognition as the path; the other is to take direct valid cognition as the path.

Inferential valid cognition is cultivated by following the traditions of the middle way established by the glorious protectors Arya Nagarjuna and Arya Asanga. The commentaries of Arya Nagarjuna demonstrated and established emptiness, and the commentaries of Arya Asanga demonstrated and established the lucid wisdom which is inseparable from emptiness, which is sugatagarbha or buddha nature. In their compositions and writings they clarify the Buddha's presentation of emptiness and wisdom respectively, and their traditions have come to be known as the empty of self and empty of other traditions of the middle way.

When pursuing inferential valid cognition, you analyze objects such as phenomena, the imputed self, and so forth, and you prove logically that things are empty and that your mind is empty.[26] It is valuable to do so because, when one says to a beginner, "All things are empty," this seems like a shocking and unreasonable statement. Therefore, it is of great value to be able logically to prove or establish that emptiness is the nature of all things.

We tend to experience things as though they existed. The imputed self [27] seems to exist, external objects seem to exist; therefore, to prove their nonexistence is something tremendous.

With regard to the lucidity or wisdom aspect, we do not normally directly experience sugatagarbha or buddha nature. But its presence can be logically established or proven in the same way as emptiness is established.[28]

So, in this way, through inferential valid cognition, you are cultivating the first two prajnas, the prajna or discernment of hearing and that of reflection and analysis. Through this approach, because emptiness and buddha nature can be logically established, it is quite easy to develop certainty about them.

However, while it is easy to gain certainty in this way, it is not easy to use that certainty as a basis for the practice of meditation. Therefore, when we turn to the cultivation of the third prajna, the prajna of meditation, we require the instructions of the great mahasiddhas—Saraha, Tilopa, Naropa, and so forth—which are not based on the logical proofs of emptiness contained in the teachings on inferential valid cognition, but are based on directly revealing emptiness to one's own direct experience in one's own mind. These instructions are found in the *dohas* or realization songs of the great masters, and they show us emptiness directly, rather than logically proving it.

Therefore, when we practice meditation, and specifically when we practice insight, we use the instructions of Saraha, Tilopa, Naropa, and other such great meditators. These instructions form the basis of the path that takes direct experience, direct valid cognition, as its main technique. In the words of Saraha, "Homage to the mind, which is like a wish-fulfilling jewel." Saraha refers to one's mind as a wish-fulfilling or wish-granting jewel, because the mind already contains within it all necessary qualities. It contains within it the potential for all wisdom, as all wisdom arises within the mind.

Now, often, when we talk about our minds, we do so somewhat pejoratively. We say our minds are full of defects, full of kleshas, full of thoughts, and so on. But really our minds are very precious; one's mind contains everything that one needs, all positive qualities. A person's mind is the source of all freedom and all wisdom. Therefore, it is with the mind that we are concerned when we take direct experience or direct valid cognition as the path, and the practice of insight meditation consists simply of looking at your mind, looking at and seeing your mind's nature.

The word for looking and the word for view here are the same in Tibetan. Normally, when we use the word "view" in the context of Buddhism, we tend to think of it as something that we are thinking about. In this regard we have to make a clear distinction between the view of inferential valid cognition and the view or direct looking of direct valid cognition. In the pursuit of inferential valid cognition, the view is developed by inference, by logical deductions, by thinking, "If it is not this, then it must be that," and so forth. But in the pursuit of meditation and the practice of insight we do not engage in that kind of logical analysis, and we do not attempt to infer what the mind is like. Therefore, it is important from the beginning to understand clearly the difference between the analytical approach of inferential valid cognition and the direct approach of direct valid cognition.

The view associated with direct valid cognition is looking at the mind, rather than thinking about the mind. For example, if someone were to study birds, inferential valid cognition would be like reading lots of books and articles about the behavior of birds—this type of bird eats this at such and such an age and develops such and such type of feathers; it grows in this way and to that degree, and so on. Direct valid cognition is very different from that approach. It would be like actually going out and following the birds around, watching them, seeing where they go, where they fly, how they fly and what they really look like, and so on. So in the pursuit or practice of direct valid cognition, rather than trying to infer what the mind is like, you observe directly what it is like. One looks to see what the mind is like when the mind is at rest; one looks to see what exactly is at rest and in what. Where is it resting; how is it at rest? When your mind moves, what moves? Where does it move, and so on? So, the difference between inferential valid cognition and direct valid cognition is the difference between inference and direct observation.

The practice of insight involves looking at the mind and observing the mind in various states and while it is performing various functions. Now, as we have explained, when you cultivate the practice of tranquility, you cultivate a state of stillness in which the mind is tranquil and at rest. And you cultivate the ability to be aware through watchfulness of that stillness, so that you will be aware, "My mind is at rest, my mind is tranquil," and so on. Sometimes, you also experience states of movement or mental activity, where thoughts are present within or moving through the mind.

In the practice of insight, you look at your mind in both states: within stillness and within the movement or occurrence of thought. First, you practice by looking at the mind within stillness. There are three stages to this. The first stage is to look at the mind within stillness or in the context of stillness. The second is to scrutinize what you find or what you discover in that state. The third is to identify or to have pointed out to you what in fact is there.

The first stage, looking at the mind within stillness, is practiced on the basis of your previous cultivation of tranquility. Through the practice of tranquility meditation—grasping the mind when it is ungrasped, stabilizing the grasped mind, and bringing enhancement or progress to that stabilization—you have cultivated sufficient mindfulness and alertness to be able to maintain a lucid state of shamatha or tranquility. That lucidity is necessary in order to be able to be aware that your mind is at rest. Now you look at that state of stillness or rest, and fundamentally, there are three things about it that you want to discover or observe. If the mind is at rest, it must be at rest in some medium or environment. So, where is the mind at rest? Secondly, if the mind is at rest, something is at rest. So, what or who is at rest? And thirdly, if the mind is at rest, if the mind is in a state of stillness, there must be some quality to that stillness. In other words, since you are able to say, "This is stillness and this is movement," they are obviously different; therefore, there must be some characteristic to that stillness, some way that the mind *is* that enables you to identify it.

When you are looking for where the mind is at rest and what it is that is at rest and how it is at rest, do not think, "I need to discover this." Do not have a preconception about what you are going to find or what you want to find. Also, do not think, "I must not find this," or, "I hope I do not experience it in this way." In the practice of insight, you are not attempting to improve on or in any way change or alter what your mind is. You are trying to see your mind as it is and as it has always been. This is the one thing we have never done. We have done many things, but we have always looked outward; we have always looked away from our own mind—under the simple assumption that it is there—but we have never looked at it. So, here you start the practice of insight by looking for where, what, and how the mind is in stillness. Do not think of anything that you observe as being particularly good or bad; just find out exactly where the mind is, what the mind is, and how the mind is.

Another way to look at the mind within stillness is to look to see where the mind comes from or came from, where it is at any moment, and where it goes. We assume that the mind must have come from somewhere, must be somewhere, and must be going somewhere. In this practice you attempt to observe these in direct experience. Now, do not be too quick to jump to the conclusion that the mind did not come from anywhere, is not anywhere, and does not go anywhere, just because its nature is emptiness. At this point everyone has heard that [laughter], but at this point it is just a belief. You may even have a sophisticated conceptual understanding of why that must or might be the case, but conceptual understanding and experiential realization are entirely different. Conceptual understanding is when you figure out that it must be like this, that there is no other way it can be than such and such a way . If you find yourself thinking that way, that is conceptual. Experiential realization is when you directly observe in your own direct experience what there is; so, beware of skewing your observation with assumptions or beliefs.

If you find yourself thinking, "Well, I know that the nature of mind is emptiness ; so, let's see, that means it cannot be anywhere," and so on, that is not the method here. You are simply trying to look at the mind and just see what you see. For example, look at the mind and try to see what its substance is—what is the stuff of mind? Does it have solidity? Does it have shape? Does it have color? If it has a particular characteristic, such as texture or shape or color, then exactly what texture, what shape, what color? If it does not have a particular characteristic, such as texture or shape or color, then, in the absence of that particular characteristic, what does it have? Of what does that absence of that particular characteristic consist? If the mind seems to have none of these substantial characteristics, then of what does that absence of characteristics consist? If the mind is nothing, of what does that nothingness consist? What is the stuff of that nothingness?

So, we're going to stop here and meditate a bit.

[Short meditation session with Rinpoche.]

[Dedication of merit.]

6 MORE ON THE FIRST INSIGHT TECHNIQUE, LOOKING AT THE MIND WITHIN STILLNESS

THE MAHASIDDHA NAROPA predicted to Lord Marpa, "Son, just as lion cubs do, the disciples will surpass the guru." We understand this to have been a prediction of the flourishing and the increase in clarity of these mahamudra instructions over time. The original source of these instructions was the instructions of the Indian mahasiddhas. But they taught somewhat cryptically through songs. Over time, generation after generation, these instructions have been progressively clarified. This progressive clarification, which has caused these instructions to become more and more effective, has in each case and in each generation been based upon practical experience and realization of the path. At present, the guidance texts that we use for mahamudra instruction and practice are the three books on mahamudra by the Ninth Gyalwang Karmapa, Wangchuk Dorje, of which the longest is our present text, *The Ocean of Definitive Meaning*. What is taught in this book is essentially the same thing that is taught in the original *dohas* of the mahasiddhas. However, it is taught in a very precise, clear, accessible, and gradual way, so that there is all the instruction that one needs from the very beginning. It teaches how a beginner can start the path through the practice of tranquility, what kinds of experiences are likely to arise and what needs to be done about them, and then how gradually to introduce oneself to and begin the practice of insight. These detailed instructions are very helpful in practice; there is no doubt about this whatsoever. It has been proven over time that this particular system of instruction is extraordinarily beneficial. It is not the case that it might be useful or it might not; it definitely is. This book and the system of instructions from which it arises make it very easy for teachers to point out mahamudra to students and make it very easy for students to actually practice mahamudra. The book makes the whole path very simple and streamlined and makes you independent of relying on a lot of extraneous resources. What is pointed out in this text, what is gradually introduced to the student, is what in the sutras we call "emptiness" and what in the mantra system of vajrayana we call "the wisdom of great bliss." The entire path of mahamudra is presented in full detail, from the very beginning practice of a beginner up to the full achievement of the fruition of mahamudra, called "great no-meditation." Now, while I cannot say that I myself possess great blessings that I can bestow upon you, I can say with complete confidence that these instructions are so profound that there is no doubt whatsoever that they will help you and will enable you to practice effectively, and, therefore, I am utterly delighted to have this opportunity to offer these instructions to you.

Obviously all of you take these instructions seriously enough to have made the effort to come here. Nevertheless, I still urge you to use the relatively short time we have together as fully and wisely as you can. Do not waste any of it. Remember that these instructions—whether you consider them as coming from the dharmakaya Vajradhara, as being the instructions of the mahasiddha Saraha, or as coming from some other source—are the instructions that will enable you to dispense with all fear of lower states of rebirth and all fear of cyclic existence. I therefore ask you to practice with enthusiasm.

Yesterday we mainly looked at the first technique of insight practice—looking at the mind within stillness. By looking at the mind within the state of stillness you are trying to observe the mind's nature in that state. The text goes on to clarify this practice and to discuss some of its implications. As you will see when you read it, the presentation of the implications of this practice is actually presented as questions to be posed by the guru or meditation instructor to the student practitioner. However, you can do this yourself by reading the text and honestly appraising your own experience. This is appropriate, because, after all, your own experience is not hidden from you. You yourself know best what you have been experiencing. The purpose of this assessment of experience, whether done in dialogue or done on your own, is to ascertain whether your experience is genuine or in some way faulty. This ascertainment can be accomplished quite clearly using this text. This portion of the text is as effective as if the Ninth Gyalwang Karmapa were sitting right in front of us asking us these questions himself. These particular questions are found in the forty-first teaching session.

The first question posed is, "What is your mind's nature like?" At this point you have been practicing insight meditation and looking at the mind's nature directly in the way, for example, you would watch the behavior of a bird. You have been looking to see how the mind comes to rest, how the mind moves, and so on. There are several things you might have experienced and that therefore might constitute your answer to this first question. You might say, "Well, there is nothing to find; I cannot find anything; there is simply nothing there." Or you might say, "What I experience is a kind of vague obscurity, a sort of darkness." Or you might say, "What I've experienced is lucidity, a kind of knowing."

Another question posed is whether or not there is any difference in your experience between the practice of tranquility meditation and this first practice of insight meditation. Previously, when you were practicing tranquility alone, you brought your mind to a state of rest in a natural way. Now, what you are doing in the initial practice of insight is looking at the mind within that state of rest or stillness. Is the experience of looking at the mind within stillness any different from the experience of stillness itself, of the experience of tranquility alone? It might be exactly the same; there might be no difference whatsoever, or it might be slightly different. If you say that there is no difference whatsoever, that the experience of looking at the mind within stillness and the experience of just achieving a state of stillness itself are not different, then you are still just practicing tranquility. There is as yet no practice of insight, and the text says that you need to remember that tranquility alone, while it can weaken kleshas, cannot eradicate them; it cannot generate great wisdom. So, if there is no difference between this first practice of insight and the practice of tranquility, you need to keep looking.

If there is a difference, if in your experience looking at the mind within stillness and simply resting in stillness are slightly different, then our text says you probably have a partial experience of your mind's nature, in which case you should continue in the same way.

About looking at the mind, it was written by the Third Gyalwang Karmapa, Rangjung Dorje, in his *Aspiration of Mahamudra,* "When one looks repeatedly at the mind which cannot be viewed or cannot be looked at." That line indicates that, when you look at your mind, there is no object to be seen in the visual sense of something you can look at physically. He continues, "When you do so, you vividly see that which cannot be seen." Vivid seeing is what we call insight or *lhaktong* (in Sanskrit, *vipashyana*). That which cannot be seen is the mind, which is not an object that is in any way separate from that which is looking. This kind of looking is not like looking outside yourself at trees or hills or buildings, and so on. Yet, while it is not an object to be viewed outside the looker, it can be experienced. There is an experience, which here is called "vividly seeing that which cannot be seen."

Now, when we look at the mind in this way, we are not trying to condition or alter the mind in any way. We are not trying to convince ourselves that that which does not exist, exists. We are not afraid of finding nothing and so are trying to find something. Nor are we trying to convince ourselves that that which exists, does not exist. We are not afraid of finding something and are not desperate to turn it into nothing. When we describe the mind, we have to say that it is not something in the usual sense of that word, because it has none of the substantial characteristics that we normally associate with words like "something" or "existence." But we also cannot say that it is nothing, because when we say nothing, we mean nothing at all, absolutely nothing. If the mind were nothing in that sense, then it would be an utter absence, like the absence of mind in a corpse. The mind is not nothingness.

Now, in order to attempt to communicate this state or characteristic of the mind, mahasiddhas have used different terminology. They have sometimes referred to it as the unity of cognitive lucidity and emptiness, or as the unity of the expanse and wisdom. Sometimes they simply say that it is inexpressible and beyond words. In any case, it is this nature, which cannot be easily characterized as one thing or another, that we are attempting in this practice to experience directly.

The previously quoted stanza by Rangjung Dorje goes on to say, "If you vividly see that which cannot be seen, you cut through doubt about any kind of, 'It is this,' or 'It is not this;' 'It is that,' or 'It is not that.'" The last line of the stanza, which makes it an aspiration, reads, "May I see this just as it is without bewilderment or confusion." It is appropriate to make this aspiration and to attempt to accomplish it through practice, because what you are looking at is the nature of your own mind. Your mind, which is looking, is fully capable of seeing its own nature. It is not something that is distant from you or hidden from you in any way. It is, therefore, most important to put the effort into looking at the mind in this way.

That is the first technique, looking at the mind within stillness. For some people this first technique will lead to experience of the mind's nature, and for some it will not. If it does not, then the text suggests that you allow a thought to arise. It does not matter what the thought is. It can be a good thought, a bad thought, a neutral thought, any kind of thought. When you allow a thought to arise, the first thing that will happen, the first thing you will experience, is the recognition that a thought has arisen. You will think, "Oh my mind moved; it is not at rest." And then you will recognize what the content of the thought is. It could be an angry thought, a lustful thought, a faithful thought, a regretful thought, a thought like, "Oh, I am happy," or, "Oh, I am sad," and so on. It does not matter what it is. Whether it is a thought of anger or sadness or delight or faith or any other kind of thought, when the thought has arisen and you experience the presence of the thought within your mind, look for it to see where it is. This means looking for the actual substance or stuff of the particular thought itself. For example, where is the anger? Or where is the sadness? Or where is the delight? And so on. Look to see where it actually is, and then look to see what it is. What is the actual stuff of which this anger or sadness or delight is made? What are its characteristics? Does it have a color? Does it have a shape? And so on.

Now, the thought is in a sense there, because you experience it, but when you look right at it and when you look for it, you will not find anything. Why? Because the thought is empty. Even while the thought is there, it is empty. But its emptiness in no way prevents or diminishes its vivid appearance. This is why, so long as we have not meditated in this way, we follow thoughts; because, in spite of their emptiness, they continue to appear. So when a thought of anger arises, it takes hold of us, and we become angry; when a thought of sadness arises, it takes hold of us, and we become sad. But if you are able to look at the nature of the thought, it dissolves. You are not overpowered by the apparent substance of the thought, because you see its emptiness, you see through it. So, doing insight practice in this way, looking at the nature of thoughts, can also lead to experience of the mind's nature and to identification of it.

You also can apply this technique to other types of experience or cognition than the sixth consciousness. You can also apply it to the functions of the five sense consciousnesses. For example, if you consider visual consciousness, obviously, when you close your eyes, you do not see external objects, shapes, colors, and so on. When you open them, you do. We are very used to seeing things; but exactly what happens when you see something? There is an event that we call cognition that occurs when you see something. But how does that happen, and where exactly do the object and the cognition encounter each other? Does the object in some way enter you, or does your cognition in some way flow out from you and encounter the object in its place? If you analyze this, you will see that, while you see things, neither is really happening. The object is not coming into you and your cognition is not going out to it. So, the eye consciousness sees, but it does not have a location anywhere; it seems to be nowhere. In the same way, if you scrutinize the experiences of hearing with the ear consciousness, smelling with the nose consciousness, tasting with the tongue consciousness, and feeling with the body consciousness, you will find that, while the intensity or vividness of the experience remains undiminished, you do not find anything when you look for it. The reason why you do not find anything is that the nature of the five sense consciousnesses is what we call emptiness. But the emptiness of the consciousnesses does not mean nothingness, because they are cognition, they are consciousness. So when you see something, that seeing is empty. When you hear something, that hearing is empty, and so forth. And yet the emptiness of seeing and the vividness of seeing in no way conflict with or inhibit one another. Therefore, it has been said by the learned, "While the apparent quality of appearance is undiminished, it is utterly empty; and while the emptiness of appearance is utterly undiminished, it is utterly apparent." This statement is true not only for visual appearances but also for the cognitions of all five sense consciousnesses.

Another way you can look at the mind, and you can do this in looking for any function of the mind—which is to say, you can look for the sixth consciousness or you can attempt to look for or locate any of the five sense consciousnesses—is to search through your body from the top of your head to the tips of your toes and try to see exactly where any particular consciousness is happening, where it is. You will not find any specific location for the cognition itself. On the other hand, you certainly cannot simply say, "It is nowhere," because there is cognition. Now, this has to be experienced, and the experience is very different from simply understanding it through logical analysis. Through logical analysis and inference you can determine, "Well, it must be like this; this is how it must be, because there is no other possibility." But that type of determination or certainty will not lead to direct experience.[29] The direct experience needs to be gained through the act or process of direct observation, and that is what is meant, as I mentioned yesterday, by the view of direct valid cognition, the looking of direct valid cognition.

So I am going to end this morning's instruction here and continue with the reading transmission I began yesterday.

[Rinpoche continues the reading transmission.]

[Rinpoche and students then dedicate the merit.]

7 Looking Carefully at the Experience of Not Finding Anything

This morning we continued to examine how to look at the mind's nature within stillness. Now we come to a scrutiny of that state—to a scrutiny of the nature of the mind experienced within stillness and of stillness itself. This scrutiny is necessary because we have always assumed that the mind exists, and yet we have never looked at it. When we start to look at it, we discover that we cannot find anything. Therefore, the text next presents how to scrutinize or look carefully at that experience of not finding anything. This is done within the context of what are called eleven forms of authentic mental engagement. In the practice of tranquility we found there were nine methods of resting the mind; here in the practice of insight there are eleven forms of authentic mental engagement.

The first of the eleven mental engagements is "thoroughly seeking." Thoroughly seeking means to seek very carefully and thoroughly for the mind in the act of observation: for example, to look for the mind within the body—is the mind somewhere within the body, and if so where is it?—scrutinizing carefully the body from the top of the head to the very tips of the toes, looking to see if the mind can be found in any location; to look for the five sense consciousnesses, looking to see if they exist within the body or if they exist within the objects of those consciousnesses; to look for the substantial characteristics of the various consciousnesses—do they have color, do they have shape, and, if not, what are they, what do they have? Now looking in this way, which characterizes this particular mental engagement, means trying to discover in direct observation the answer to these questions, rather than trying to figure them out or to infer them through analysis.

The second mental engagement is called "individual scrutiny." You can think of it as detailed scrutiny, because it involves being very precise and very detailed in your scrutiny of mind and mind's functions. Sometimes you apply this scrutiny within stillness; you look at the mind itself within the state of stillness. And sometimes you apply this scrutiny within movement or the occurrence of thought, and in that case you can analyze the thoughts that arise. Again, analyze here means direct observation and not coming to conclusions about the thoughts. When you scrutinize thoughts, you look to see if you can observe an origin from which the thought comes, a location where the thought abides while it is present, and a destination to which the thought goes after it has dissolved or disappeared. Look to see if you can find an environment or container that supports or contains the thought.

Now, this does not involve inference of any kind. It is not a matter of thinking, "Thoughts must be like this; they must come from here or go to there." It is a matter of direct observation, and that observation must not be impeded by easy assumptions or habitual thinking or attitudes. For example, if you are looking at a thought of anger and you ask yourself the questions, "Where did this anger come from, where is it, where is it going," normally, we would simply say, "Well my anger arose from my conflict with such and such an enemy; as for where it is, it is right here; and as for where it is going, it will go wherever anger goes, where it will be ready to come back any time someone gives me trouble." That is not what we are looking for here. Here we are looking for direct observation of the very stuff or substance of anger, the very nature of the anger itself, to watch and observe where it comes from, where it is, and where it goes. That type of careful scrutiny is what is called here individual examination or individual scrutiny.

The third mental engagement is called *shibmor chöpa*. *Shibmor* means "in great detail" or "very, very precisely" and *chöpa* is the strongest form of the word that means "to examine, analyze, or scrutinize." So, in your notes make a distinction between the second and the third. Although the difference between them is not clear in the name, there is a very clear difference between them. In the second mental engagement, individual scrutiny, you were mostly looking at objects of mind such as thoughts. Here you turn the same type of scrutiny in on itself, and you look at that which has been looking. You look at that which has been seeking for the existence or nonexistence—or whatever—of the object. So the difference between the second and the third is that in the case of the second you are looking at objects of mind and in the third you are looking at that which experiences objects of mind, at that which is looking, at that which has been performing the scrutiny.

Now, this kind of careful looking at both objects of mind, as in the second engagement, and at mind itself, as in the third, is very important, because sometimes it seems to us as if objects of experience exist and that which experiences exists. So therefore, it is important to scrutinize, to examine carefully and thoroughly, both of these. When you look at them, you find that there is nothing there.

The fourth mental engagement is called "tranquility," and it is the same word, *shamatha* or *shinay*, that is used to describe tranquility meditation. Here it has a more specific meaning. Through the first three mental engagements, through the thorough scrutiny that has been developed during those first three engagements, it has been resolved that objects of mind and mind itself are not to be found, and that the not-finding-anything when you look for the mind is not because you have failed to find it; nor is it because the mind exists but is somehow too subtle to be found in that way; nor is it because it is too far away from you, too distant to be seen—after all it is your mind. The reason that you do not find anything is that in not finding anything you are finding what the mind is, which is emptiness, and this is a matter of direct experience. In the fourth mental engagement, you rest your mind in that direct experience, applying the faculties of mindfulness and alertness that you developed during the previous practice of tranquility meditation.

Now, the difference between tranquility as the fourth mental engagement of insight practice and tranquility meditation per se, which we studied earlier, is simply that, when you practiced tranquility before, you had not seen your mind's nature. You were just resting in it, but it was unseen. Here, having seen the mind's nature, you rest in it, but you are resting in a lucid certainty, an experiential rather than conceptual apprehension of that nature. So therefore, it is a state of tranquility or shamatha but it is tranquility with a difference.

The fifth mental engagement is called "insight" and here it is the same word, *vipashyana* or *lhaktong*, which is used for this entire practice of insight. Through the practice of the fourth mental engagement, which is tranquility, you have practiced resting your mind in the recognition of your mind's nature. Nevertheless, the lucidity on which the recognition depends continues to require some reinforcement. Therefore, in order to further generate or further reinforce or strengthen that lucidity, it is important not just to rest in an already gained recognition of the mind's nature, but repeatedly and actively to look again and again at that nature. For example, in *Moonbeams of Mahamudra,* Dakpo Tashi Namgyal says that, when you practice insight, if you just practice insight alone, somehow the stability of the lucidity of insight can diminish, and that can inhibit progress. Therefore, he says, even when you are practicing insight, you need to be careful to maintain the active or vigorous quality of mindfulness and alertness. In this connection, in describing his own experience, he uses the words, "a mindfulness and alertness that are both clear and sharp." So this means that even at this point you must not simply rest in the nature of mind passively; there still needs to be the intentional application of this effort of mindfulness and alertness in looking at or scrutinizing the mind. This is of particular importance because of what is called the undercurrent, which is a continuous undercurrent of subtle thoughts, which, if unrecognized, can weaken the lucidity of insight and the stability of tranquility. So, the point of this fifth mental engagement is that, even when you are resting in the recognition of mind's nature, it is important within that resting to look at or scrutinize that nature again and again in order to generate the necessary lucidity.

The sixth mental engagement is called "unity," which here refers to the unification of the fourth mental engagement, tranquility, and the fifth, insight. Up to this point you have cultivated both the lucidity of recognizing mind's nature through the practice of insight as a mental engagement and the stability or stillness of resting in the recognition of mind's nature through the practice of tranquility as a mental engagement. Now, obviously, since these occur within the generic context of insight meditation based upon tranquility meditation, the two are very closely related. Nevertheless, even at this point they can sometimes seem somewhat contradictory. Sometimes in experience they can inhibit or interfere with one another. You may have the experience that sometimes, when the lucidity of recognizing mind's nature—the aspect of insight—is strongest, it somehow causes the tranquility or stillness of resting in that recognition to be weaker. And sometimes you may have the experience that when the tranquility or stability of resting in the recognition of mind's nature is most stable and possesses the greatest quality of stillness, the actual lucidity of the recognitions seems somehow diminished by it. So here, as the sixth mental engagement, you are practicing the unification of these two, tranquility and insight, so that they no longer interfere with or inhibit one another. In the end, you must bring them to the point where the stability heightens or strengthens the lucidity and the lucidity stabilizes the stillness.

The seventh mental engagement is called "lucidity," and the eighth is called "no conceptuality," and the two are best thought of as a pair, because they correspond to one another, although they serve different functions. You will remember from the instruction in tranquility meditation that the greatest obstacles to meditation are torpor and excitement. These are obstacles not only to the practice of tranquility but also to the practice of insight, and therefore, at this point in one's practice, if they are occurring, they must be corrected. The seventh mental engagement, lucidity, is the remedy for torpor, and it is to do anything appropriate that enhances the mind's lucidity and dispels torpor. Even at this time, if you wish, you may employ the mahabhrama samadhi, which was taught in the context of tranquility meditation, or use any other means which serves to dispel torpor, to promote enthusiasm, and thereby to enable you to continue the practice with the necessary lucidity.[30]

The eighth mental engagement, "no conceptuality," is the remedy for the other major problem in meditation, which is excitement, in which your mind is distracted by pleasant, unpleasant, or neutral thoughts. You may employ at this time, if you wish, the subterranean samadhi, which was presented previously in the section on tranquility as a remedy for excitement, or any other suitable method that will dispel the problem of excitement so that you can remain in samadhi.[31]

The ninth mental engagement is called "equanimity," and is connected with the idea presented in the common vehicle of avoiding the extremes of excessive unconcern and excessive concern. Excessive unconcern is when a defect is present in meditation, either torpor or excitement, and you fail to apply the appropriate remedy. But excessive concern is when the defect is not present, and there is no problem, but you worry about the possible arising of such a defect. You think, "Oh, maybe I am going to become torpid or maybe I am going to become excited." This anxiety or excessive concern about the possibility of a defect arising in the future is itself an obstacle to meditation. So the practice of the ninth mental engagement is, once the defect has been dispelled—for example, torpor by the seventh mental engagement or excitement by the eighth, then not to continue to apply the remedy. Once it has served its purpose you return in equanimity to the prior practice and do not speculate about the possible recurrence of that defect in the future.

The tenth mental engagement is called "no interruption," and it refers to the continuation or continuity of practice. It means that you do not discard your meditation through undervaluing it or through regarding it as useless. This needs to be stated, because otherwise it might happen that you practice with diligence for a time, and thereby generate authentic experience, but then somehow discard the practice. There will be no progress if that is done. It is important to continue with the practice. Now this tenth mental engagement refers to continuity or continuation primarily in the context of even placement or meditation practice.

The eleventh and final mental engagement, called "no distraction," refers primarily to the practice of post-meditation or subsequent attainment.[32] It sometimes happens that we are diligent in even placement, in meditation practice, but when we arise from the meditation session, we think, "Now I can relax," and we let go in the wrong way and our thoughts run wild. This is a serious impediment to progress. Therefore, the eleventh mental engagement, no distraction, is to maintain, as much as possible, the faculties of mindfulness, alertness, and watchfulness in post-meditation—to recollect frequently the lucidity and stability of the meditation practice and attempt, as best you can, to bring it into your daily activities such as working and eating and talking. Now, obviously, this is somewhat difficult in the beginning, but if you try to do it repeatedly, it will become more and more possible. By maintaining mindfulness in post-meditation, your meditation is enhanced, and your meditation in turn facilitates the easy application of mindfulness in post-meditation. That is the eleventh and final mental engagement, which is called no distraction.

The practice of insight through the application of these eleven authentic mental engagements is the cultivation of direct observation of the mind and not the cultivation of conceptual understanding of the mind. There is a great difference between these two, and this difference is crucial to the practice of mahamudra. For example, if you look at a painting with your eyes, you see the colors of the paint; you see yellow and red and blue and whatever. Thereafter, at some point you can also close your eyes and imagine or recollect what you saw. In the language of valid cognition, what you actually see is the thing itself and what you recollect is a generalized abstraction of the thing; it is a general image that is based upon but is not the thing itself. The distinction between the direct experience of a thing and the entertaining in the mind of a generalized abstraction of that thing is very important. The danger of not understanding the distinction between understanding and experience is that your mahamudra practice can degenerate into speculation, in which the sixth consciousness, which after all is in its main function conceptual, will think about mind, think about itself, think, "It must be like this, it can be no other way than this," and so on. And because the ideas that you might entertain in that way are in some cases valid, and in the context of theory even useful, you may think that you are having meditation experience. But in fact, the generation of understanding cannot serve in the place of meditation experience. It does not have the power to eradicate bewilderment in the way meditation experience and direct experience of the mind does.

When we talk about direct valid cognition, the most common example used is sensory direct valid cognition—for example, when you look at something with your eyes and see it. However, in this case, when we are talking about direct valid cognition of the mind's nature we obviously are not talking about physically seeing something. In the study of valid cognition, four types of direct valid cognition are mentioned: sensory direct valid cognition, mental direct valid cognition, self-aware direct valid cognition, and yogic direct valid cognition. Self-aware direct valid cognition is simply your mind's capacity to know what it is experiencing at any time. It is always there, although it is generally somewhat unclear to us, as we pay very little attention to it. For example, the sixth consciousness does not directly experience any object of the senses, but instead generates a generalized abstraction that is a replica or image of something that was experienced by one of the sense consciousnesses.

Nevertheless, while the sixth consciousness, the mental consciousness, cannot experience an object of the senses directly but only as an abstraction, it can experience itself directly. It is, in the language of valid cognition, not concealed from itself. So therefore, it is possible to have direct experience of your own mind. In this case, in the case of mahamudra, the particular type of direct valid cognition that is being used is the fourth type, yogic direct valid cognition. This refers to authentic direct experience or direct valid cognition of the nature of your mind, and it is utterly different from conceptually understanding the nature of mind. It is absolutely necessary that the distinction between understanding and experience be clear to you.

I am going to stop here for this afternoon, and if there are any among you who wish to ask questions, please go ahead.

Question: Thank you, Rinpoche, for the wonderful teachings; we are very fortunate. My question has to do with something you went over yesterday, the self-liberation of thoughts. I wonder if you could help us with how to know whether or not we have actually experienced that. Is it when a thought arises in meditation, and it may be a thought that in some way is bothersome to you, but having recognized that the thought is there, it does not return? And can one consider that experience validated if in post-meditation you find that bothersome thought also seems not to be present any longer? Perhaps both of these ideas are wrong. So, I would just like some help with this. Because we hear the phrase "self-liberation" so often, there would seem to be a danger in telling ourselves, "Oh, great! I recognize the thought, so now it is liberated; how wonderful!" But that may indeed not be the case.

Rinpoche: What you are experiencing both in meditation and post-meditation is a type of self-liberation of thought. In fact, for a thought to be considered to be self-liberated, it does not necessarily follow that it will not reoccur. The self-liberation of a thought does not necessarily entail the permanent liberation or permanent cessation of that type of thought or that particular content. It means that a thought dissolves without your having to get rid of it intentionally, because you see its nature. In the beginning, even after one is able to see the nature of thoughts, and is able thereby to allow them to dissolve naturally, they will reoccur, but over time they will become weaker and weaker and will reoccur less and less.

Question: Rinpoche, my question is in regard to the third category of the tranquility section, enhancing stability. In my reading of that section, my impression was that one uses the sense perceptions and the occurrence of thought in order to reestablish the stillness of tranquility, and in your explanation of it, it seemed to be a bit different than that and had more to do with a kind of a continual watchfulness, particularly during the post-meditation state, as opposed to accomplishing a more intense experience of that stillness again and again. So I wonder if that is correct, if I am interpreting that correctly.

Rinpoche: Well, they are basically the same thing put two different ways, because, if the faculty of watchfulness is cultivated, then tranquility meditation transcends any type of suppression of experience through regarding it as a source of disturbance, and therefore, it is somewhat connected with post-meditation, and is connected also with appearances and thoughts.

Question: The specific instructions Rinpoche gave were to be in the state of mind of knowing that you are looking at something and knowing that you are thinking. So there is obviously a mindfulness of immediate experience or of quality to that experience, but to me that is not exactly the same as stillness, the moment of stillness in the mahamudra practice itself.

Rinpoche: I do not completely understand the distinction you are making, but in my opinion, the third set of tranquility instructions is primarily concerned with post-meditation because in the first two parts, grasping the ungrasped mind and stabilizing the mind that has been grasped, you are cultivating stillness through the practice of even placement, and in the third part, enhancement or progress upon stabilization, you are attempting to use the situation of post-meditation and the application of the watchfulness of mindfulness and alertness in post-meditation to stabilize that stillness.

Question: Rinpoche, my question is about devotion. You have said that devotion is the most important factor in cultivating direct looking at our mind. Is that [devotion generated] before we are actually looking, so that we get the enthusiasm and confidence to do the practice, or, while we are actually looking, is there a warmth or a connection that we can experience that can help us?

Rinpoche: You do not consciously try to cultivate devotion while looking at the mind. You consciously cultivate it before looking at the mind and after looking at the mind, and through having that devotion and through repeated supplication [of the root and lineage gurus and/or of yidams], your devotion affects your practice while you are looking at the mind. From one point of view, devotion causes you to have more trust and confidence in the instructions, which makes you more diligent and concentrated in your application of them. But it does more than that; devotion alters how you experience things. For example, when people feel strong devotion, sometimes they will cry or they will get goose bumps and so on. These things indicate that their state of mind is somehow altered, and that alteration of the state of mind can make you more receptive to unfabricated experience and to recognition of the mind's nature.

Question: Rinpoche, in the mahabhrama samadhi, in which you visualize the white small pea-sized sphere of light going up, is this something that you said you use as needed? So would this be one shot, and then does this light stay up there? Or would you repeat this a few times in a session? Exactly how do we use this?

Rinpoche: It does not really matter. First you try doing it once and then direct your mind to the sphere of light that you are at that point visualizing very high in space, and if that is enough to dispel your torpor, then you would return to the main technique. If that is not enough to dispel the torpor, then you can do it again and again. That is okay, too.

Question: In this process of looking, the scrutiny, when you have some direct experience that there is nothing there to find, you follow with the next step of insight of "I've looked; I've seen there is nothing there; therefore, I'll keep looking; therefore, I'll relax; therefore, I'll let go." I am just not sure what you might say to yourself, the next non-thought . . . [laughter]

Rinpoche: This is discussed in the text when the student is asked, "What do you see when you look at your mind." If they say, "Nothing at all; there is nothing there," that means that they have partially seen their mind. This is called a partial seeing. The mind has two characteristics, emptiness and cognitive lucidity. When you see nothing at all, that is seeing emptiness, but it is not enough, because you have not recognized the cognitive lucidity. It is not enough, because the mind is not nothing. If the mind were nothing, then the whole world would be nothing; there would be no experience. If there were nothing, we would just be like corpses. So there is a cognitive lucidity to the mind, and that has to be recognized in the same way. So, if you are seeing nothing, you need to go back and look again, and you can read about this in your book.

Question: Could Rinpoche say something about time, particularly in the phase when one is looking at the mind and going back and forth between looking at the mind between the thoughts and the mind having the thought?

Translator: About time?

Question: Yes.

Translator: This context?

Question: I had a feeling that was coming. I could ask it in a different way maybe. Is the experience of looking at one's mind outside of time? Or is even the activity of doing that equivalent to time?

Rinpoche: When you are looking at your mind, this activity is not happening in a state beyond or without time. The function or action of mind that enables you to look at your mind is what is called "the awareness of now, awareness of the present." You will remember that in the first instructions on tranquility meditation it said, "Do not prolong the past, do not beckon the future, rest in awareness of the present moment without conceptualization." That resting in the awareness of the present moment of experience continues in the practice of insight. When you are looking at your mind, what is looking is called an ordinary cognition of now or of the present. Now, through doing this, eventually you will see that time is nonexistent, but that will not happen now; that will happen later.

In somewhat more detail, when you look at your mind, the mind that you are looking at is the mind of now. When you are looking, it is the mind of now, because there is no other mind for you to look at. The mind of the past has ceased to exist; the mind of the future has not yet come into existence. So the only mind that is an object of direct valid cognition is the mind of now. Therefore, it is not happening beyond time; it is happening in the present.

Question: The times when I actually think I am looking at my mind, and I am experiencing that, I often have physical sensations that in the past I've always not really tried to do anything with. But it happens so much, and it feels like tightening. Now it seems like my throat and my jaws often tighten, so my ears go bad or something. And I wonder am I straining? I do not know if it is really a valid experience, or if it is something I am forcing myself into thinking. Am I deluding myself into thinking it is a valid experience, or should I consciously really try to relax?

Rinpoche: It is not uncommon for practitioners, especially in the beginning, to have the experience that concentrated attention of mind will produce physical tension, and what you have to learn to do, ironically, is to separate your mind and body. In other words, teach yourself to be focused with your mind without becoming physically tense. Probably the best way to begin to do this is to practice some tranquility meditation at the beginning of the session, and at that point in the session do not try to look at your mind using the methods of insight. Now you will probably find that, as a result of the habit that you have built up, even when you practice tranquility meditation, you may find yourself physically tightening up. If so, while maintaining the proper focus of mind for tranquility meditation, consciously relax your body. Put some time and effort into relaxing, especially the muscles of the limbs. And then, when you have gotten to the point where you can maintain a focused mind with a relaxed body, then return to the practice of insight. And even while you are doing the insight practice and primarily looking at mind, from time to time during the session check to make sure that you are physically relaxed, and if you are tense, then take some time to consciously relax. It has been said traditionally that in the beginning we need to learn to combine mental focus with physical relaxation, and that does not really happen automatically; it has to be practiced.

[Rinpoche and students dedicate the merit.]

8 WITHIN STILLNESS, LOOKING, SCRUTINIZING, IDENTIFYING AWARENESS/EMPTINESS

CONTINUING FROM where we left off yesterday, we are still in the section of insight instruction called "looking at the mind within stillness." Within this section there are three sections: looking, scrutinizing, and pointing out or identifying awareness/emptiness. Yesterday we finished the first two of these sections. Today we are going to begin with the third section, identifying awareness/emptiness.

First of all, it needs to be kept in mind that all things, as individual things or phenomena, possess individual characteristics. For example, the characteristic of earth is solidity, the characteristic of water is wetness, the characteristic of fire is heat, and so forth. In the same way, the defining characteristic of mind or of cognition is cognitive lucidity or awareness. So when definitions of things are given, it is said that the definition of mind or cognition is cognitive lucidity. However, in another respect, mind, which has this defining characteristic, is quite different from most other things. External things such as earth and water and fire and so on, have the appearance to us of solidity and external existence, but when you consider your mind, while it does have its obvious characteristic of cognitive lucidity, its nature is fairly obviously emptiness. For this reason, in the tradition of the mahasiddhas, the mind rather than external phenomena is taken as the basis of meditation.

In order to establish or determine the emptiness of external phenomena, because we do not experience them as empty but rather as being solid, logical analysis is needed. And even when, through rigorous logical analysis, you have proven to yourself that external phenomena are empty, that emptiness is still not a direct experience. Even after you have proven to yourself that they lack solidity or solid substantial existence, external phenomena appear to have solidity; you still perceive them in that way. Therefore, although, through the reasonings of the middle way school, you can develop an inferential certainty that all things without exception are empty, it is very hard to apply that in the practice of meditation. For that reason, the path of the sutras[33] is said to take three periods of innumerable eons, during which the accumulations of merit and wisdom have to be accumulated gradually, and that buddhahood can only be attained through that path in that way, because it is only through the force of such a massive accumulation of merit that inferential understanding can be used as a basis for the gradual development of true experience.

For this reason it has been recommended by all mahasiddhas not to take external objects, external phenomena, as the basis of meditation, but to take cognition itself as the basis of meditation. The reason for this is simply that, when you look at your mind, you can directly experience its nature. It is not concealed from you in the way the emptiness of other phenomena is. The problem is that we have never looked at the mind, and that is what has kept us from seeing its nature; but if you look at your mind, you can and will recognize that its nature is emptiness.

Now the term emptiness or shunyata in any language gives rise to the connotation or image of nothingness. But the emptiness of nothingness is very different from the emptiness of all things or the emptiness of the mind. Nothingness is completely dead, a complete vacuum. The emptiness of all things, however, is not nothingness; it is interdependence. It is the unity or sameness of the appearance of something and its emptiness, the unity or sameness of the lucidity or vividness of something and its emptiness. When you look at your mind, you do not find anything, and the reason you do not find anything is that the mind's nature is emptiness. But the mind is not just empty; while being empty, its characteristic, its defining characteristic, is awareness. Therefore, when the mind is described, terminology like the unity of cognitive lucidity and emptiness or the unity of awareness and emptiness is used. Unity here is meant very strongly. The nature of awareness is emptiness, and the nature of the mind's emptiness is awareness. This can be revealed to you in your own experience through looking at the mind.

Though it is true that the path of the sutras requires three periods of innumerable kalpas, it is also taught that through the vajrayana path you can achieve the state of great unity, the state of Vajradhara, in one life and in one body. Now, when you think of the path of the sutras and how long it takes, it sounds utterly impossible that you could achieve the same thing in one lifetime, because if that were true, then clearly the path of the sutras would be unnecessary. However, both are correct; both are true, and the difference is the difference between the absence and the presence, respectively, of the practical instruction of the mahasiddhas to take direct experience, direct valid cognition of the mind, as the path.

When you take looking directly at your mind as the path, you can achieve the state of Vajradhara in one lifetime, and this has been accomplished by the mahasiddhas from whom these instructions have come. It is also true that the great bodhisattvas have gathered the accumulations over three periods of innumerable eons.[34] And it is also true that the result of these two approaches is exactly the same. Therefore, we employ the practical instruction of the mahasiddhas, which in essence is to look at one's mind to recognize in direct experience the mind's nature, its emptiness; to recognize in direct experience its lucidity; and to recognize the unity of these two.

Now, when you are meditating by looking at the nature of your mind, you are not attempting to create or alter that nature in any way. This nature is not something that you can create through the practice of meditation. It is not something that is bestowed upon you by the Buddha. It is something that has always been there, has always been your nature, but because we normally never look at it, we have never seen it. If you look at it, you will see it and you will recognize it.

Therefore, in *The Ocean of Definitive Meaning* it says, "Rest the mind naturally and in a relaxed way. Within that state of relaxation look nakedly and vividly at the mind." Now nakedly here means without any kind of barrier between that which is looking and the mind that is being looked at, without any kind of filtration such as a skin or packaging. You are not packaging the mind with ideas about it; it is naked or unwrapped. And looking vividly means that you are looking at it right now with the awareness of right now as a vivid direct experience, something that is clear and present to you right now, rather than considering the mind and thinking about the mind that was or the mind that will be.

Further the text says, "And look in this way, nakedly and vividly, without distraction." This means that while remaining relaxed, you remain undistracted from direct observation of your mind.

The nature that you experience when looking at your mind in that way is what we call buddha nature, which, as the Buddha taught in the final dharmachakra, is something that each and every being possesses. Buddha nature does not need to be created, it is not bestowed upon us by anyone; it is what we possess innately. About buddha nature it is said in the *Uttaratantra Shastra*, "There is nothing in this that needs to be removed. There is nothing that needs to be added to this. When you look at that which is genuine in a genuine way and you genuinely see it, you will be liberated."

When it says that there is nothing in this that needs to be removed, it means that there is nothing in the nature of the mind that is inherently defective in any way; therefore, there is nothing you have to try to get rid of. There is also nothing lacking in the nature of mind; there is nothing else that needs to be introduced or added to it. All that needs to be done is to see that true or genuine nature—what your mind truly is—to see it properly by looking at it in the right way, by looking at it in a way free of concepts. So by looking in a genuine way at that genuine or true nature, there is no doubt, you will see it genuinely as it is, and that in itself will bring liberation. Therefore, the practice is to relax the mind utterly and yet to remain undistracted from the direct experience or observation of it.

The method of meditation explained at this point is to be free of any kind of alteration—not to alter the mind, but to look at the nature of the mind, to allow the mind to look at its own nature. So be free of alteration and look at your own nature. Being free of alteration also means not having any particular expectation of certain types of experience and not wishing for certain types of experience. For example, you will remember the rainbow meditation, which was described earlier—not wishing for that type of experience.

With respect to resting the mind within observation, it was said by Saraha, "If water is undisturbed, it is clear; if it is shaken or agitated, it is unclear. If a lamp flame is undisturbed by the wind, it is bright, but if it is blown about by the wind, it is unclear." So here the instruction is to rest the mind completely within the act or context of the mind observing its own nature. This will engender both lucidity and stability.

About meditating in that way our text says, "Do not look elsewhere." You are not attempting to look outside that which is looking, nor is this a meditation of not knowing; it is not a meditation of ignorance or absence of recognitions. Rest in awareness in the present instant. Rest in the awareness that is there in the present instant that is awareness *of* the present instant. In order to do this our text says, "Sometimes tighten up; sometimes use more exertion. Sometimes loosen up; sometimes relax; but always be without distraction and maintain continuous mindfulness."

In more detail the text advises, "During even placement, during meditation, relax the mind; and during subsequent attainment, during post-meditation, tighten up the mind." The reason why you need to put more exertion into post-meditation mindfulness is that post-meditation by its nature involves lots of potentially distracting factors, such as complex actions and activities, conversation, the need to think about things, and so forth. Therefore, it is recommended that you tighten up your mind in post-meditation and relax it in meditation.

This section of our text, the identification or pointing out of awareness/emptiness, has one practice session—the practice itself is not further subdivided—but three teaching sessions. After the first teaching session and the single practice session there are two more teaching sessions, which discuss the implications of this particular pointing out. Brought up again is the possible problem of mistaking understanding for experience, and again it is stressed that we need to gain direct experience, not conceptual understanding. In addition it is mentioned that there are three ways that genuine insight, *lhaktong* or *vipashyana,* can arise in this context. One way is called the arising of insight within stillness or nonconceptuality. This occurs when your mind is at rest and still, and within that stillness of mind you recognize the mind's nature. For some people that does not occur; they do not recognize their mind's nature within stillness, but they are able to do so within the occurrence or presence of a thought. So for some people, when a thought arises, they are able to recognize the nature of that thought and, thereby, the nature of the mind. What is recognized is the same, whether the insight arises within stillness or within occurrence. In either case, what is recognized is the unity of cognitive lucidity and emptiness.

Now for some people neither of those insights occurs, but insight arises in a different way, called the arising of insight within appearances. In this particular context, appearances refer specifically to the generalized abstractions that the sixth consciousness generates based upon sense experience. Based upon any one of the five sense consciousnesses, the sixth consciousness can, does, and will generate generalized abstractions that we normally take to be the external object that is perceived by that particular sense consciousness. Whether it is a generalization of form or a generalization of sound, it is the sixth consciousness' generalized abstraction of the sense experience, and it is, therefore, in and of itself, not an external object. These generalized abstractions that are experienced by the sixth consciousness are not true external objects; they are projections of the sixth consciousness, and therefore, in a very true sense, they are the mind arising in that shape. They are the mind arising as that apparent form or as that apparent sound, and so forth. So therefore, when looking at these generalized abstractions that arise within the sixth consciousness, if you observe their nature—that they are apparent, that they do appear, that you can experience them, but that they are utterly empty—then their nature is seen to be that same unity of cognitive lucidity and emptiness, and their nature is also seen to be mere interdependence. So if this is directly recognized, this is also a genuine insight. Therefore, there are three different ways according to our text that insight may arise at this point, and they are all equally valid.

I'm going to stop there for this morning and continue with the reading transmission.

[Rinpoche continues the reading transmission.]

[Rinpoche and students dedicate the merit.]

9 LOOKING AT THE MIND WITHIN THE OCCURRENCE OF THOUGHT

THIS MORNING we finished the section of this book called, "looking at the mind within stillness." Now we turn to the second section of insight meditation practice, which is "looking at the mind within the occurrence of thought." Since, by the time one has first arrived at the point of practicing insight meditation, one has already practiced tranquility meditation assiduously, the first technique presented in this section on insight is how to look at the mind within stillness. But if or when one is unable to gain insight through that method, the second technique, how to look at the mind within the occurrence of thought, is needed. In this book there are three ways that you are taught to look at your mind: looking at the mind within stillness; looking at the mind within the occurrence of thought; and looking at the mind within appearances.

In a shorter text on mahamudra, also by the Ninth Gyalwang Karmapa, called *Pointing Out the Dharmakaya*, these three and then two additional methods of insight meditation are taught: looking at whether the body and the mind are the same or different; and looking at whether stillness and occurrence are the same or different.[35] Thus five methods are taught. Here only three are taught. In fact, any one of these may be sufficient for an individual to develop recognition of the mind's nature. And if recognition of the mind's nature is gained through any one of these methods, that is sufficient. Alternatively, you may practice any two of them, or if you wish, all three.

According to the study of cognition, as it is found in our texts, the sixth consciousness, the mental consciousness, does not actually directly experience any of the objects of the senses. The objects of the senses are, however, directly experienced by the five sense consciousnesses—although obviously each of these is limited to the experience of its particular object. So the eye consciousness does directly see forms, the ear consciousness does hear sounds, and so forth. These are direct experiences. What the mental consciousness does is to generate an image of what the eye has seen, what the ear has heard, and so on. The sixth consciousness does not and cannot experience any of the five sense objects directly. But it does generate an image. That image is a generalized abstraction, which means that it is not as clear as the actual sense experience. It is somewhat vague.

This is true of the mental consciousness' experience of all the five senses. Based on the direct experience of these senses, the sixth consciousness generates a generalized abstraction or abstracted image of visual form, an abstracted sound or an image of physical sound, and the same thing with smells, tastes, and tactile sensations. None of these abstractions that are generated by the mental consciousness are as clear as or as well-defined as the actual experiences of the senses that they seek to replicate.

The sixth consciousness is confused. It mistakes or confuses its abstractions for the actual objects of the senses. It treats its abstractions as though they were the objects of the senses. The sixth consciousness, the mental consciousness, regards its abstractions—based on physical form—as physical form; its abstracted images of sound as actual sound, and so forth. In the context of the study of valid cognition, an image for how all of this works is given. The five sense consciousnesses are said to be like a mute person who can see. This person can see and, therefore, can experience, but not being able to speak, cannot describe or communicate anything that they experience. The sixth consciousness is said to be like a sightless person who can talk. The sixth consciousness cannot see anything, but if it does find out about something, it can talk about it all and at once. And of course, as we know, this is precisely what the sixth consciousness does. It thinks, and in thinking, it mixes things up. It treats the past as though it were the present, it treats the future as though it were the present, and in that way expects the present to be what was there in the past, and so on.

In any case, it is clear, through this analogy, that the five sense consciousnesses and the sixth consciousness have no way to communicate with one another directly. The medium of communication between the five sense consciousnesses, which, according to the analogy, cannot talk, and the sixth consciousness, which cannot see, is self-awareness. Self-awareness, which is another faculty of mind, forms the bridge or medium between the five sense consciousnesses and the sixth consciousness.

Now all of this is theoretical, but it provides a background for understanding what you are doing when you practice looking at the mind within occurrence. When you look at the mind within occurrence, you allow your mind, the sixth consciousness, to generate a thought. The first type of thought that is mentioned here is an abstraction—an abstracted or generalized image of something that is familiar to you. Suggested in the text are such things as the *Jowo* image of the Buddha in Lhasa, or the Tsurpu *Hla Chen,* another great statue of the Buddha, which was, at the time this text was written, at Tsurpu. But it could be anything. It should be something familiar to you. You could imagine your home or part of your home or something you own—for example, your automobile. When you imagine your car, the image arises more or less vividly to your mind. Look at that image. Try to determine what the relationship between the car and the mind is. Has your car entered your mind? Has your mind gone to where your car is? If you scrutinize this you will see that nothing like that is happening at all. The image, while being apparent and vivid, is utterly nonexistent.

It is not the case that it is impossible for your automobile to appear as an image in your mind; it does appear there as an image. And of course that image is a generalized abstraction. Nevertheless, when you look to see where that image of the automobile is, if you look to see if it is inside your body, or outside your body, it does not seem to be anywhere. Nor has your mind become that automobile. Nor has that automobile become your mind. While the image is present in your experience, it has no existence whatsoever. This is the unity of cognitive lucidity and emptiness in the context of the occurrence of something within your mind. By looking at images generated by your mind, you can start to recognize the emptiness of whatever occurs to or within the mind. The emptiness, however, of such an image, in no way diminishes or contradicts the vividness of appearance or presence of the image in your mind. And recognizing this in experience is the first step in recognizing the mind's nature within occurrence.

The second practice in this section of looking at the mind within occurrence, and the thirty-ninth practice session presented in our text, is concerned with the intensity of thought. Previously, when you looked at the mind within stillness, you were looking at a mind that was tranquil, and therefore, not particularly intense. When you look at the mind within the occurrence of thought, you have the opportunity to look at it when it is very intense. Therefore, the second practice in this section concerns using those types of thoughts or occurrences within the mind that are the most intense—states of delight and misery. As we all know, sometimes our minds are filled with delight and sometimes we are miserable—we are sad, we are depressed, and we are regretful. In both cases, what characterizes the mental state and what is common to both is the intensity of what is occurring within the mind. Normally, we make a great distinction between delight and misery. When we feel really happy, we like that, and we regard states of sadness and unhappiness and feeling regretful as extremely unpleasant. But if you look at what is occurring in your mind in either case, you will see that the nature of it, the stuff of which it is made, is no different from the nature of the mind itself. And in that sense, the occurrence of either delight or misery is like the appearance of waves on the surface of an ocean. For example, when you are experiencing delight in your mind, there is certainly an experience, because you are aware of it. But when you look for its substance, its nature, its essence, you find that there is nothing there. Or, when you are intensely sad, even miserable, if you look at the nature of the sadness or misery, then you will see that, while the sadness is there as a vivid appearance, just as the mind itself has no substantial existence, in the same way, the sadness has no substantial existence.

It is very easy to understand this. It is important, however, not to jump to the conclusion that these things have no existence. You need actually to look for yourselves and find it out directly. And when you are looking, you have to look with an open mind, without anticipating what you are going to discover. However, eventually you will find that there is nothing to be found. And once the sensation or the occurrence of delight or misery has been found not to be found anywhere, it will dissolve. First, you try this with delight or happiness. You can practice when naturally experiencing a state of delight, or, if you are not naturally experiencing one, try to think of something delightful.

Then, once you have seen the nature of feelings of delight, then try it with feelings of misery and sadness. If you do not naturally have these feelings, then think of something that makes you miserable. In both cases, when you look at the occurrence, you will see that it is empty—just as the mind itself is empty. It is like a mirage or an illusion. It is like froth that is churned up on the surface of the water. Some of these emotions we experience as intolerable, such as intense regret, for example. But, when you know how to look at the nature of what occurs in your mind, you do not need to attempt to block these types of emotions, because by looking at them and seeing their nature, they will dissolve of themselves.

The first practice session of looking at the mind within occurrence was looking at the nature of a generalized abstraction arising within the sixth consciousness. The second was looking at the nature of delight and misery. The third is looking at the nature of kleshas or mental afflictions.[36]

For example, when something pleasant, something desirable, comes to mind, we generate craving and attachment, we generate desire. When something unpleasant, something to which we are averse, comes to mind, we generate aversion [and sometimes even anger and hatred]. Sometimes, reflecting upon our own amazing qualities or great power, we generate pride. Sometimes, reflecting upon the qualities, and so forth, of others, we generate jealousy. And sometimes we feel greed for what we possess and the need to hold on to it. All of these types of mental afflictions or kleshas are disturbing to us. So long as we look away from them when they arise and look outward at the objects that form the condition for their arising, we are overpowered by them.[37] The solution is to turn inward and look directly at the klesha itself, rather than at the object with which the klesha is concerned. You turn inward and look to see where the klesha, the thought that has the content of klesha, is, what its nature is, where it came from, where it remains, and so on. You will not find any of these things. For, just like delight and misery, kleshas are empty. We have been enslaved by our kleshas for no other reason than that we have been unaware of their emptiness. The enslavement is unnecessary and will end when you *experience* their emptiness.

Sometimes you can overcome kleshas in this way. Sometimes you will look at the nature of a klesha and it will dissolve. And sometimes you will not be able to do so. This is not because any of these kleshas has true existence. It is because we have the strong habit of being ruled by them. If you cultivate the opposite habit, the habit of looking at their nature, as that habit through repeated cultivation is reinforced, the instances of recognition will increase and the instances of being overpowered by the klesha will decrease. It is possible to cultivate this habit for the simple reason that kleshas are empty. They have no true existence. It was for this reason that, when the Buddha taught the *Heart Sutra,* he said, "No form, no sensation, no perception, no mental arisings, no consciousness, no eyes, no ears," and so on. When, by looking at the nature of a klesha, you see this in direct experience, the klesha is pacified. However, that pacification or liberation of that klesha is not permanent. That particular thought dissolves, but it will reoccur—again, not because the kleshas have true existence, but because we have the habit of allowing their reoccurrence and of entertaining them. In the sutras it is taught that the cultivation and habituation of this type of remedy forms much of the practice of the path of meditation—the idea of meditation being related to the idea of cultivation and habituation. The point is that by becoming more and more used to the remedial action of seeing the nature of kleshas, the kleshas themselves will become less and less powerful and finally will be eradicated.

There are three practice sessions in the section that is called looking at the mind within occurrence. The first was looking at the mind within arising in the sixth consciousness of a generalized abstraction; the second, looking at the mind within delight and misery; and the third, looking at the mind within the arising of kleshas or mental afflictions, such as any of the three or five poisons.[38] These three practice sessions are enumerated in the text as the thirty-eighth, thirty-ninth, and fortieth practice sessions.

A similar idea to looking at the mind within occurrence is found in dzogchen empowerments, in which you are often told, "Send your mind to the east. Does it go anywhere? And is there anything going there? Send your mind to the south. Does it go anywhere? And is there anything going there?," and so on. You are instructed to send your mind out to the four directions and then to look at the experience of doing so. This is essentially the same idea as looking at the mind within occurrence.

Following these three practice sessions, and given to support these three stages of practice, are two further teaching sessions. To begin with, these are concerned with how we relate to thoughts. Usually, as meditators, we regard thoughts as something unwanted. We do not want thoughts to arise because we view them as impediments to meditation. Here, because thoughts are an opportunity to look at the mind, thoughts are not regarded as a problem. Whatever arises in the mind is treated equally. You simply look at its nature, even if it is a klesha. By looking at its nature, it is self-liberated. Even if it is intense delight or misery, it is self-liberated when its nature is seen. It does not interfere with meditation. And even the arising of an image or generalized abstraction in the mind can be self-liberated as well.

It is, therefore, of some importance that we learn not to regard thoughts as a problem, not to regard thoughts as enemies, but to regard them as supports for meditation. About this, Lord Gampopa said, "See thoughts as necessary, as valuable, as helpful, as kind, and cherish them." The kindness of thoughts, the value of thoughts, is that they reveal our own nature, mahamudra, to us, which is a great help. Obviously, if you follow thoughts, if instead of looking at their nature you follow them, then that will impede meditation. But if you see their nature, and the thoughts are self-liberated, that is a great help. Therefore, Gampopa said, "If you know how to rest within whatever thought arises and it is therefore self-liberated, then, since that itself is the dharmakaya, they are indeed worthy of being cherished. If you do not have this attitude, if you do not regard thoughts as opportunities for insight, meditation becomes very difficult and inconvenient, because it becomes a battle against thinking, which among other things, makes the meditation unclear and unstable."

Speaking to his students, Gampopa also said, "Meditators seem to want to have no thoughts, but they cannot stop thinking, and therefore they become exhausted. However, even if a lot of thoughts are present within the mind, this is not a problem as long as you can look at and see their nature. Therefore, it is appropriate to abstain from any attempt either to get rid of or to follow thoughts."

The presentation of the reason why it is important to take thoughts on the path is the fiftieth teaching session. It is not a separate practice session, as it does not introduce a new practice. The fifty-first teaching session presents various questions that are to be posed, and the point of these questions is to ensure that the practitioner is not mistaking conceptual understanding of the nature of thoughts for actual experience of the nature of thoughts, because conceptual understanding will not weaken or eradicate mental afflictions.

I have something to say about the use of the terms "tranquility" and "insight," or "shinay" and "lhaktong," "shamatha" and "vipashyana." Traditionally, mahamudra instruction and, therefore, mahamudra practices are divided into these two classifications. The distinct instruction in mahamudra always includes instruction in tranquility and instruction in insight. However, many other meditation systems use these same terms. The terms "shamatha" and "vipashyana" are used not only by most Buddhist meditation systems, but by other Indian systems, including some Hindu traditions. The reason for this is that all of these traditions at some point have used Sanskrit, and therefore the original terminology with which they speak of meditation tends to be very similar. Within the Buddhist tradition, the Theravadan tradition—which uses Pali, a language very similar to Sanskrit, as its scriptural language—also calls its meditation practices "shamatha" and "vipashyana." And then we have the mahamudra practices of shamatha and vipashyana—which, as we know, were named by the mahasiddhas who codified them.

Now, do not think, just because all of these different systems call their various mediation practices by the same name, that these are in fact the same practices. They are not. The methods of shamatha and vipashyana, and therefore the results of shamatha and vipashyana in Hindu meditation systems, Theravadan meditation systems, and the mahamudra meditation system, are all different. For example, the shamatha or tranquility techniques taught here—grasping the ungrasped mind, stabilizing it once it has been grasped, and bringing progress upon stabilization—are unique to mahamudra. And also the vipashyana or insight practices of looking at the mind within stillness, looking at the mind within occurrence, and looking at the mind within appearances are also unique to mahamudra. They are different from the similarly named techniques found in Hindu systems, Theravadan systems, or in other Buddhist traditions. Of course, the nature with which we are concerned is the same, but how we look at it is very different.

In mahamudra we are concerned with the intense and precise scrutiny of the mind. The purpose and result of mahamudra meditation is that through such scrutiny we come to recognize the mind's nature, which is dharmata, the nature of all things, and thereby to achieve all wisdom and all qualities. The purpose of mahamudra tranquility meditation is to bring about the immediate pacification of the kleshas; and that of mahamudra insight meditation is to bring about the ultimate eradication of the kleshas, through which the wisdom of the Buddha is realized.

I'm going to stop there for this afternoon. Now we will meditate.

[Rinpoche and students meditate and then dedicate the merit.]

10 LOOKING AT THE MIND WITHIN APPEARANCES

THERE ARE THREE different approaches to insight practice that are presented in this text on mahamudra: looking at the mind within stillness; looking at the mind within occurrence; and looking at the mind within appearances. The point of presenting three techniques is that any particular individual may respond more to one of these three approaches than to the others. In *Pointing Out the Dharmakaya*, five approaches, including these three, are presented. Of these three presented in *The Ocean of Definitive Meaning*, looking at the mind within stillness is presented as the main one. The other two—looking at the mind within occurrence, and looking at the mind within appearances—are presented as supplements to that. That is why, if you look at the outline of your text, you will see that, although we would think of looking at the mind within appearances as the third section, it is called the second. It is called the second because it is the second supplement to the first section. Here calling it the second section means that it is the third [laughter].

Even though it is, in a sense, supplemental to looking at the mind within stillness, looking at the mind within appearances is presented here somewhat elaborately, which means it is divided into four practices and four presentations: seeing appearances as mind; seeing mind as emptiness; seeing emptiness as spontaneous presence; and seeing spontaneous presence as self-liberation.

Before I start to explain the first of these, seeing appearances as mind, I would like to relate something about my own experience of these ideas, simply because I imagine you may have undergone this yourselves. When I was quite young and began to study texts, the first thing about emptiness that I encountered in my study was the presentation of the selflessness of persons. When I first studied this, I thought it was ridiculous, because what was being said to me was that mind did not exist. I thought, "Well, that is weird. I know my mind exists." But when I analyzed my mind, according to the reasonings presented in the context of this study, the reasonings that have been produced by the various scholars and siddhas, I became certain in the sense of conceptual understanding that the personal self does not exist.

Then, when I went on in my studies and was exposed to the idea that not just the personal self but all phenomena lacked true existence in that same way, I first thought, "Well, it is true that the personal self does not exist; this has been proven to me. But to say that all things are empty is going too far. After all, I see things, I hear things, and so on. How can these be nonexistent?" Then when I encountered the reasonings of the middle way school, and they were explained to me by my tutors, I realized that I had been wrong. It was true that all phenomena lacked true existence. At that point I developed certainty based upon a theoretical conceptual understanding of the selflessness of persons and the selflessness of phenomena.

Then I started to be advised by some of my teachers that theoretical understanding alone—which makes you, in pejorative terminology, what we call a thinker or speculator—was not enough. They began to encourage me actually to look at my own mind without analysis, and they said, "If you look at your mind, good experience, direct experience, is possible."

When I started to look at my mind, I became convinced that emptiness is not something distant from us. It is not something that we have to turn outwards to discover. It is always potentially available to us as a direct object of experience. What I am saying to you is that these doctrines are not mere superstition. They can actually be validated through your own direct experience of them. I mention this because, on the face of it, these four statements—appearances are mind; mind is emptiness; emptiness is spontaneous presence; and spontaneous presence is self-liberation—may sound somewhat grandiose and unverifiable. But if you actually go through these practices you will be able to experience the truth of these assertions on your own.

The first of the four stages of looking at the mind within appearances is seeing appearances as mind. When the subject of the relationship between mind and appearances is presented using inferential valid cognition, we return to the basic format of the Buddha's three dharmachakras. As you know, the Buddha taught in three distinct phases, which we call the three dharmachakras. Subsequently, the teachings given in that way were formalized or codified by scholars and siddhas as what we now call the four systems. The four systems—called the vaibhashika, the sautrantika or sutra system, the chittamatra or mind only, and the madhyamaka or middle way—are not really understood as different systems, but as different stages of subtlety or profundity in the presentation of the buddhadharma. The first, the vaibhashika, is designed for beginners; the second is more profound; the third more profound than that; and the fourth more profound than the third. They can be divided in different ways. The first two systems, the vaibhashika and the sautrantika, have in common that they assert the true existence of external objects. The second two, the chittamatra and the madhyamaka, have in common that they assert the nonexistence of external objects. Here we are talking about understanding, rather than realization. We are talking about a conceptual view.

Because of the progressive refinement of these four views, we generally use the first three systems—the two which assert the existence of external objects, and the third, the mind only school—to describe how things appear, which we refer to as relative truth. And we use the fourth, the middle way school, to describe how things are, which is absolute truth.

The first of the two schools that assert the existence of external objects, the vaibhashika school, has a quite rough or coarse assertion of reality. They, and the sautrantikas, do assert or accept the existence of external objects. However, they do so in a particular way. Essentially what they say is that what we see—mountains, buildings, and our own bodies, etc.—are not merely projections of our mind. These things actually exist externally, but not in the coarse way that they seem to, not as what we see them to be, but as subtle particles. So, according to the vaibhashikas and the sautrantikas, the subtle particles, which are the building blocks of physical phenomena, have true existence. Coarse appearances, according to these schools—in other words, the appearance of things that are made up of particles but appear not to be made up of particles, but to be solid units—these coarse appearances are mental designations, based upon the experience of things that are really just made up of particles. To put this clearly, a mountain, according to the vaibhashikas and sautrantikas, is not really one thing. We designate it as one thing with the concept, mountain. It is actually many things. It is made up of many, many subtle particles. In the same way, your body is not one thing. Your body has parts: a head, a trunk, and four limbs. Even if you select one of the limbs—for example, your hand—your hand is not one thing. It has many parts: the five fingers, the palm, and so forth. Even if you select one of these five fingers, such as the thumb, the thumb is not one thing. It has three joints. (Translator: "Mine only has two. [laughter] Anyway, it has some joints." [laughter])—And then if you select any one those joints, that joint is not one thing, because it consists of skin and flesh and bone and muscle, and so forth. If you continue this mode of analysis, eventually you get to the point at which the only things that you can say that exist, according to the vaibhashikas, are the subtle particles of which all of these physical substances are made. Therefore, they say that the entire world is made up of particles and that the particles truly exist, but that the coarse appearances that we designate, based upon the presence of the particles, do not.

The vaibhashika and sautrantika presentation of the true existence of subtle particles, and, therefore, the existence of external objec ts, is the same. They differ, however, in their presentation of how external objects appear to us—in other words, as to what we are actually seeing when we see something. The vaibhashikas say that objects are external to us, and that they exist because they are made up of particles. Mind cognition, they say, is internal, And what happens when you experience things—for example, when you look at columns, houses, mountains, or different colors—is that you are actually seeing them. The object is out there and it exists; you are in here, your cognition functions, and you experience it. In other words, the vaibhashikas' presentation of perception is very much the way we normally think of it.

But the sautrantikas dispute this. The sautrantikas say that the defining characteristic of cognition, that which experiences, is cognitive lucidity, the capacity to be aware. The defining characteristic of external objects, which they assert to exist in the sense that they are compounded of subtle particles, is matter. They say that matter and cognition are of utterly different natures. Therefore, the sautrantikas say that, when you see something, you are not actually seeing the thing itself. You are seeing a mental image of it. According to the sautrantikas, in any act or event of perception, what is actually happening is that your mind is adopting the form of the object. The sautrantikas assert that the object exists externally; it is composed or compounded of particles. In the very first instant of contact with the object, the characteristics of the object are perceived. But in the second instant, what you experience is a mental replica, or a mental similitude, of the object. So, according to the sautrantikas, what we see and hear, and so on, is mind, not the object.[39] But, they also say that the objective basis, in the language of the sautrantikas, the hidden objective basis for that [entirely mental event of perception], does exist externally. For, example, when you look at a mountain, according to the sautrantikas, what you are seeing is not the mountain, but your own mind. However, the mountain does exist. The mountain is the hidden objective basis which serves as the cause for your being able to see the mental replica of a mountain. According to the sautrantikas, the relationship between truly existent external phenomena and the displays of mind that we experience is one of cause and result.

So, according to the sautrantikas, appearances are half mind and half not. What we see, what we experience, is mind, but the basis of seeing, the basis of that experience, is not mind. It is external. In his presentation of valid cognition the great master Dharmakirti taught that the sautrantika view is a very useful way to consider external phenomena and our relationship with them. About this he said, "When you look outside, you must mount the stairs of the sautrantika system, because it is a very appropriate and convenient way to evaluate your relationship with external phenomena."

As much as the sautrantika way of describing experience is valuable, when we actually consider the status, from their own side, of external phenomena, we tend to resort to the third system of tenets, which is the mind only school. The mind only school differs from the sautrantika in that it does not accept the existence of the objective bases of appearances. There are two parts to their presentation of this. According to the mind only school, the sautrantika description of experience as the appearance of mind in the guise of external phenomena, is very good. But one of the bases of that assertion, that there is an objectively existent external phenomenon as which the mind masquerades, is disputed by them. The mind only school says that it is unfitting or unreasonable to assert the true or absolute existence of the hidden objective bases of perception. They say that one reason why it is unfitting to do so is that it is unreasonable to assert that such an objective basis could somehow cause the mind to generate a replica of the objective basis. The mind only school says that as a description of relative truth it is useful to talk about particles, because, of course, it can be determined that substances are indeed made up of particles. What they dispute is that if you assert that these particles have a degree or status of existence greater than that of the coarse substances which are made up of them, you must be asserting that the particles or some component of the particles is truly indivisible.

According to the mind only school, if you analyze particles, no matter how subtle in detail this analysis becomes, you always find parts. Every particle always turns out to be made up of smaller particles. And no matter how long you continue to divide them with your mind, you never get to the end of this. No matter how many steps or stages down the way you go in your analysis, you never seem to find something that is not made up of at least two parts [like a right side and a left side, or a top and a bottom]. Even if, theoretically, you were to find a particle that could not in any way be physically reduced to smaller components, and it were in some physical way truly the smallest existent thing, there would have to be more than one of them to make up coarse physical objects. Otherwise, there could be no appearances of coarse, visible objects, since such objects could obviously not be made up of one particle. So if there were more than one particle—let us say if there were two of them—then they would have to be in some locational relationship to one another. That would mean that there would be a surface on each particle, or part of a surface of each particle, that would be facing the other particle, and a surface that would be facing away from that particle. Of course, there would be more than that, but we are keeping it simple for the sake of discussion. In that way each particle would have to have at least two parts. It would have to have a part facing the other particle and a part not facing the other particle, which would mean that it was not truly partless. According to the mind only school, it is true that particles exist as the building blocks of phenomena, but they exist as relative truths. They do not exist as absolute truths.

The mind only school's basic criticism of the sautrantika assertion of external objects as truly existent because they are composed of particles which are indivisible is that all particles, no matter how subtle, are aggregates, and, therefore, not indivisible. They can always be further divided. This assertion is presented in detail, using the argument of the different faces or surfaces which a particle must have to have a certain identity in relation to other particles. For example, one argument is to imagine three particles that have a certain relationship with one another. We could say that there is one toward the east, one in the middle, and one toward the west. Well, if there is one in the middle, between two other particles, then it must have an eastern face and a western face, by the very fact that part of it is facing the east and part of it is facing the west. Therefore, any particle must have at least two identifiable parts. Through this type of reasoning, the mind only school comes to the conclusion that it is impossible to assert the true and independent existence of external objects on the basis of their being composed of particles, because it is impossible reasonably to assert the true and independent existence of particles, since they are themselves aggregates.

So, the first argument was the refutation of the sautrantikas' assertion of truly existent particles. The second is their assertion of the centrality of cognition. This has two parts: the assertion of the nature of experience, and the assertion of the unity of experience. The mind only school's assertion of the cognitive nature of experience is, simply put, that our only reason for asserting the existence of anything is that we experience it. We only come up with the idea that the mountain exists, because we see it. The only proof of things is experience. At some point, proof has to be based on experience. And experience, by definition, always occurs within the mind.

Their second argument, the unity of experience, is that, if what we see truly exists external to our minds, then it should continue to appear independent of a mind, independent of a perceiver. And yet, no one has ever experienced anything without their experiencing it. There can be no appearance without a mind to experience it. In short, the only basis for the assertion of existence is appearance; and the only possible context for appearance is a mind to which something appears. The mind only school admits that, when we look at something like a mountain, it does seem to be outside of ourselves, and that we, therefore, assume that it is outside of our mind, but in actual fact it is appearing within our mind. It is an experience that takes place within our mind.

For example, when you are dreaming, say the chittamatrins, you might dream of a house, and in the dream you seem to be *inside* the house. But in fact, the house is *within* your experience of it and, in that sense, within your mind. When you dream you seem to inhabit a body, and yet that body in the dream is within your experience within your mind. It is much the same way in the waking state as well; everything that we see, everything that we experience, regardless of whether it seems to be internal or external, is within the sphere of our experience—and therefore within our mind.

All of these arguments and proofs involve inferential valid cognition, and constitute the reasons that the first three systems of tenets respectively have given for considering appearances to be mind. Especially important among these are the reasonings of the third system of tenets, the mind only school. However, the question remains: If that is true, why do we experience things the way we do and why do we experience things at all? For example, when you look at a mountain, it is huge and impressive. It does not *seem* as though it is within your mind or within you at all. But according to the mind only school, we experience what we do and the way we do because of habits that have been established in the all-basis consciousness. For example, when you are dreaming, the basis of the dream images is your daytime experience. In the same way, according to the mind only school, the basis of experience is not a hidden objective basis, as asserted by the sautrantikas, but the habits within the all-basis consciousness. It is therefore called a subjective basis. If you consider what happens when you dream, as you go to sleep, the undercurrent of thought starts to turn from being simply thoughts into being progressively more and more vivid images. These are experienced, of course, by the sixth consciousness. Nevertheless, according to valid cognition texts, during the dream state the sixth consciousness functions somewhat differently from the way it functions in the waking state. You remember that in the waking state the sixth consciousness only experiences generalized abstractions based upon the sense experiences. In the dream state the sixth consciousness actually experiences the images within it directly. And these images, which are vivid similitudes of sense experience, are therefore not thought of as generalized abstractions. They are thought of as a dream state equivalent to sense experience. In the context of dreaming, within the sixth consciousness, all of the functions of the five sense consciousnesses are duplicated in a way that they are not during the waking state. Of course, these are not true sense consciousnesses, in that the sense organs are not functioning, as they do during the daytime. A duplicate set of the five sense consciousnesses, pertaining to the sixth consciousness, is functioning. Therefore, because of their functioning, appearances resembling those of the five senses occur during dreams.

Those are, briefly put, the arguments for the assertion that appearances are mind. And all of that, of course, involves inference. Now, we turn to direct experience. What is presented at this point in our text is how through meditation direct experience appears as mind. This has three sections: two practice sessions, and one teaching session. The two practice sessions are the two parts of working with the relationship between appearances and mind. The first is looking at appearances and discovering them to be mind. The second part is looking at the body and discovering it to be mind. And then there is one teaching session, which provides support for these two practices by discussing the reasons why this experience or insight is valid by quoting the songs of mahasiddhas.

The first practice is concerned with appearances in the sense of external objects, what we normally would regard as outside of ourselves. The practice is to look directly at an external object. When you look at an external object for a long time it becomes unpleasant. You really get tired of looking at it. You want to stop; your eyes start to sting or smart. But if you look directly at the object without any kind of prejudice or reservation about what you are going to discover, you will become aware that what you have regarded as an external object is merely an event within your eye consciousness or an instant of eye consciousness. What you are experiencing does not exist out there; it is not an external event. It is an event of the eye consciousness. Nevertheless, it continues to appear vividly in the way that it normally does as though it were physically external to you.

The second part of the practice is to look at your body in the same way and to scrutinize the relationship between mind and body and to ask yourself several questions: How are the body and mind really connected? What is the true relationship between them? For example, is there such a thing as a mind apart from a body, or a body apart from a mind? Does the mind inhabit the body? Or is the body merely an appearance within the mind? Our text tells us that if you pursue this meditation of scrutiny then you will experience directly that the body is really an appearance to and within your mind. Those are the two practice sessions.

If you practice these meditations, you will experience these things. But if you find it very difficult to do, if you find this approach difficult, then for the time being you can limit your meditation on appearances to the abstractions or generalizations that arise within the mind. In other words, if you do not wish to contemplate the nature of external phenomena in this way, you can simply consider or scrutinize the nature of what the sixth consciousness perceives, because that is also an aspect of appearances.

I'm going to stop there for this morning and continue with the reading transmission.

[Rinpoche continues with the reading transmission.]

[Rinpoche and students dedicate the merit.]

11 THE ACTUAL MEDITATION ON THE RELATIONSHIP BETWEEN APPEARANCES AND MIND

T HIS MORNING we looked at the first of the four stages of pointing out the mind within appearances—pointing out that appearances are mind. I began by explaining the positions and arguments of the first three of the four systems of tenets[40] about the relationship between appearances and mind. Once I had finished doing that, I started to explain the actual meditation. Because at that point there was not much time left this morning, this explanation was somewhat brief, for which I apologize.

To continue, when you look at a form as we normally do, generally speaking, what seems to be happening when you see something is what the vaibhashikas say is happening—that your cognition, which is internal, is somehow experiencing or contacting an object that is external. But if you keep on looking, you start to notice that that is not really what is going on. If you can continue to rest within, for example, the experience of looking at an object of visual perception, you realize that what is happening is not so much the mind contacting something outside itself, as it is the mind acting like a mirror which reflects an image of something. In that sense, the image is contained within the mind. So when you actually look at what you are looking at, you realize that you are still looking at your mind. This is what we call "seeing." This is something that you can gradually realize through your own experience and through your own practice.

The mind is not really going out to an object. Nevertheless, because we have the habit of treating the act of seeing,[41] for example, that way, when we see something, we are unclear or confused about exactly what is occurring. We are unclear about where the action of the eye consciousness ends and the action of the mental consciousness begins. For example, when I hold up this stick of incense, and you look at it, simply seeing the incense—seeing this piece of incense without appraising it as one thing or another—is an action of the eye consciousness. Then, when I hold up a slightly longer one, you decide that the first one is short and the second one is long. There being two, you naturally compare them one to the other. Normally we make no distinction in perception between simply seeing something and making that kind of decision or designation about its qualities or characteristics. The conditional nature of that designation becomes obvious when I put down the first stick of incense and pick up another one that is longer than the second one, because then the second one, which a moment ago you thought was the long one, now becomes the short one. This means that it is not inherently long or short. These are designations which the mind, specifically the mental consciousness, generates on the basis of the eye consciousness' seeing the sticks of incense.

To use another example for how the mind generates appearances: in front of me on my table, there is a cup, which I can see and presumably you can see, too. To describe that thing that is in front of me on my table we would use the word "cup." But the sound "cup" has no inherent connection to the thing itself. They are not the same. The word "cup" is a sound. The thing, cup, is in this context a visual form, something we see. And yet, if someone says, "cup," we automatically assume that they are talking about a thing that is a cup. But there is no inherent connection between the sound "cup" and the thing that we call a "cup." The connection is made, based on habit and our mental association. Our mind, in that case, generates the appearance of that thing as what we think of as "cup."

The other aspect of looking at the relationship between appearances and mind is whether the body and mind are the same or different. Normally, we tend to think of them as different. Most people have a vague idea that their body is like the dwelling place of their mind—as though the body were the house and their mind were someone living in that house. In fact, they are indivisible, because the mind pervades the body. For example, if a thorn is stuck into your head and you say, "I feel that in my head," what you mean by saying that you feel it is that your mind experiences this sensation. It happens to your body, but it is experienced by mind. If the thorn is stuck into your foot, then you feel it in your foot, which means that your mind experiences what is happening to your body. If the body could experience things alone, without the mind, then if you stuck a thorn into a corpse it would feel it, which it does not. The mind and the body together are what enable you to feel things physically. This means that your mind is in no way separate from your body. The two are inseparable.

What is most important about recognizing appearances to be mind is not what it says about appearances but what it says about the mind. That with which we are principally concerned is the mind. Therefore, what follows is the second pointing out, which is pointing out the mind to be emptiness.

Normally, we think that our minds are in some way solid, which means that they really exist. The easiest way to think about the question of the mind's true existence is with the reasoning about one or many, which is a common argument found in the middle way school. The basis of the argument is that for something to exist it must be one thing. If it is an aggregate, if it is made up of many things, unless all of those many things truly exist, it does not exist. It was for this reason that the Buddha introduced the concept of aggregate, such as the five aggregates: the aggregate of form, the aggregate of sensation, the aggregate of perception, the aggregate of mental arisings, and the aggregate of consciousness. The basic idea of aggregates is that something that is made of many things does not have true existence.

If we look at the mind, it becomes very difficult to assert the unity of the mind when you consider its functions, which are after all its defining characteristics and the only basis for asserting its existence to begin with. For example, the eye consciousness and the ear consciousness, while both being consciousnesses, cannot duplicate or exchange one another's functions. The eye consciousness cannot hear, the ear consciousness cannot see. Therefore, they cannot be said to be the same thing because their characteristics are different. Or if you consider the sixth consciousness and any or all of the five sense consciousnesses, their characteristics are different enough that you cannot say that they are all one thing. Furthermore, even within one consciousness, because one consciousness in some way contacts or entertains variation, even one consciousness cannot be said to be a true and indivisible unit. If we use the eye consciousness as an example of this, the relationship between the eye consciousness and its object is explained differently in different contexts by different schools. For example, it is taught that in the appearance of an eye consciousness, in the occurrence of an act or event of visual perception, there are two focuses that occur. There is the external referent, which is the apprehended external object. And then there is the internal referent, which is the appearance of an apprehending cognition. There is the external object and the inner basis, at least in how things appear.

If you think about what it means to look at something, for example, at the brocade that decorates the table in front of me—it is multicolored, and it has a fairly complex weave or pattern, there are several different explanations about what happens when you look at it. One explanation is that while the external referent, the object, is variegated, the cognition that experiences is not. According to that explanation, the subjective aspect of the eye consciousness can somehow scan while being one thing, can scan or take in many different things—the variegation of the weave in this case. Another explanation is called the split egg explanation, which is that neither is, in fact, variegated. It is the quickness of the scanning that allows for the appearances of variegation. In other words, the object that you are actually seeing is being seen only one part at a time—and your mind assembles that one-part-at-a-time-seeing. In the initial seeing, the subject and object in each instant of seeing are equally unitary, and then the mind assembles a picture of their variegation. A third explanation is called equal variegation, which is that in order to perceive variegation, the perceiving cognition must also possess variegation. According to that explanation, cognition itself becomes a degree of variegation equal to the object that it is experiencing.

The assertion that appearances are mind is properly an assertion of the mind only school. The assertion that mind is emptiness is properly an assertion of the middle way school. The middle way school begins by saying it is fine to say that appearances are mind. But it is not fine to say that the mind exists. According to the middle way school, the belief that the mind exists is mistaking the appearance of continuity for existence. Continuity in this case means that what we call a mind, anyone's mind, is believed to exist because it stretches from an apparently infinite past all the way to the present. And it stretches from the present into the unforeseeable future. When we think about time, we can think about it in any way we want to. We can think about it in relatively long terms—like the past as last year, the present as this year, and the future as next year. Or we can think about it in shorter terms and say that the past is last month, the present is this month, and the future is next month. Or we can say that the past is yesterday, the present is today, and the future is tomorrow. Or, the past was this morning, the present is now, and the future is this evening. Or, the past is the previous moment and everything that went before that; the present is now; and the future is the next moment and everything that will occur after that. Everything that is past, from the previous moment and every other moment that came before that, going back infinitely, does not exist; all of that is gone. Everything that is in the future, from the next moment onward, does not yet exist. All that exists is whatever exists now. But what is the duration of now? Either now has duration or it does not. If is does not have duration, it is unreasonable to say that it exists. If it does not have duration, it is merely a hypothetical boundary between what is past and what is future. If it does have duration, how much duration does it have? Whatever unit of time you select to designate as now, you will see that half of that unit of time is past and half of that unit of time is future. No matter how finely you scrutinize time, you will see that what we call now has no duration. That means, among other things, that every thought you ever had is gone. And the thoughts that you have not had yet, of course, have not appeared yet. So right now your mind has no duration. According to the middle way school, this is why it is unreasonable to say that the mind exists. Because the time in which it might exist does not exist. We designate it as existent based upon the belief in the existence of time, and, therefore, continuity.

That is the argument that is the basis for the assertion that you cannot assert that the mind exists. In meditation, of course, we do not entertain the argument. We simply look directly at the mind. As we saw earlier, when looking directly, you do not find any thing. What you discover is the mind's emptiness. Therefore, it has been said, "It is not something and is not seen even by the victors."[42] This is pointed out, because when you look at the mind and do not find anything, your first reaction may be to think, "I don't know how to look," or, "I'm not looking hard enough," or, "I'm not smart enough to find it." The point is that no one will ever find anything; even the victorious ones, the buddhas, when they look at the mind, do not see anything.

So, I am going to stop there for this afternoon, and if you would like to ask any questions, please go ahead.

Question: Hello. I have two questions. As I was having dinner before I left for this retreat, I was sitting next to a friend of mine who is really intelligent but doesn't know anything about the dharma at all. He asked me where I was going, and I said I was going on a retreat to study a text called *The Ocean of Definitive Meaning*. He looked at me and said, "What exactly does that mean?" And I said that that was beyond the scope of that discussion. Could you give a really brief explanation of what the title, *The Ocean of Definitive Meaning*, means?

And my second question: A couple of times during this morning's teachings you said, "If you look at your mind, there is no doubt that you will see its nature." Is that you who is saying so, or is the Ninth Karmapa saying that? And if you're saying it, where does that come from, that there is no doubt? Because I first got instructions on looking at the mind three years ago at the Catherine Blaine Elementary School at the mahamudra teachings you gave there and I've been trying to look at my mind. It's not that there's been no kind of experience, but nothing that I would say is definitive. If these instructions are so straightforward, why in all of this looking . . . ?

Rinpoche: To answer your first question first, the word, *dön*, that gets translated as "meaning" in *The Ocean of Definitive Meaning* can also mean "purpose." It means the "point" of something. Everything that we do has a point.

For example, if we make a cup of tea, the point is to be able to drink tea. If you go to the market, the point is to be able to buy whatever you want to buy. Here, the point or purpose or meaning of this book is something tremendous. It is something that is definitely, absolutely, certainly important and useful. In the context of this book, it is best to think of the definitive meaning as something that is absolutely and vitally important and worthwhile. "Ocean" here means something that is really big. Since something like two thirds of this planet's surface is covered by ocean, ocean is just about the biggest thing that we know. When it is called *The Ocean of Definitive Meaning*, it means that this book contains a lot of really useful "stuff." [laughter]

Translator's aside: Laugh now, because you may not find it funny when I continue to translate.

Rinpoche: Now, about your second question: The statement that, if you look at your mind's nature, there is no doubt that you will see it, comes from me personally, because I think you will. You said that you have been looking at your mind for the last three years, that you received instruction in this practice three years ago. This is a good opportunity to talk about this, because we were just talking about time a minute ago. Three years sound like a long time. Three years contain roughly a thousand days and a thousand nights. I presume that you were not looking at your mind while you were asleep. So, in fact, you were not looking at your mind for three years; you were looking at your mind for a year-and-a-half. [laughter] So then...

Translator's aside: Wait it gets much worse. [laughter]

Rinpoche: Then, let us be optimistic and say that, at the most, you might have been looking at your mind for twelve hours a day. That is equivalent of a year-and-a-half. But I suspect that you were not looking at your mind for twelve hours every day for the last three years. So when you actually figure out how much time you really spent looking at your mind, probably it was not very much. [laughter] And that is why you have not seen it yet. [laughter] So...

Translator's aside: It sounds terrible, but...

Rinpoche: So, if you really do look at it, you will see it.

Questioner: I mean, let's say it was only three hours between now and then; let's say it was just since this morning.

Translator: Sure!

Questioner: I mean why does there have to be a duration of looking?

Translator: Right! Okay!

Rinpoche: There is no reason. [laughter] Your mind is not something that is far away from you or distant from you. So there is no reason whatsoever for not being able to see it right away. Probably in those three hours most of the time you were thinking about what you were going to eat or what you were going to drink or how much you had eaten or how much you had drunk. Probably very little of the three hours was actually spent looking at the mind.

Question: Rinpoche, you have spoken about mahamudra meditation and investigations in relation to the first six consciousnesses. What is the relationship between mahamudra practice and experience, and the seventh and the eighth consciousnesses? That is my first question.

Rinpoche: The five sense consciousnesses and the sixth consciousness, the mental consciousness, are called "clear and fluctuating" consciousnesses, whereas the seventh and eighth consciousnesses are called "unclear, stable" consciousnesses. Clear means that they are obvious to us in our experience; we can perceive their functions. Fluctuating means that they stop and start. They have functions; they are not merely a constant presence. Unclear means that the seventh and the eighth consciousnesses are very difficult for us to perceive directly. And stable means that their functioning is a stable, subtle presence rather than a fluctuation of function. For this reason, in the first turning of the dharmachakra, the Buddha only described the first six consciousnesses and did not mention the seventh or eighth. Later on of course, he did describe them. When you are practicing meditation, it is easier to work with the six consciousnesses because they are more easily available to you as objects of scrutiny. You may in time come to recognize the functions and experience the presence of the other two consciousnesses as well. But it is not necessary to be concerned with them because the meditation based on the six consciousnesses is held to be sufficient.

Same questioner: The insight part of the text talks about looking and pointing out. Does that imply that in order for the pointing-out section to be of actual use it must be pointed out directly by a teacher?

Rinpoche: The idea behind this is that the actual instructions for practice are presented as looking at the mind. And then the determination of the quality of experiences and the resolution of the experience gained through looking at the mind are pointed out through pointing out. What I have been doing here is presenting the sections on looking at the mind because I feel that the pointing-out sections are in a sense not as necessary, because you will gain the experience through looking, and if I were simply to do the pointing out, it would be kind of "macho" or presumptuous.

Translator's aside: It's a funny word, *chok chok*. It's almost like saying "macho," except it's not gender specific. But it's kind of like "presumptuous," maybe.

Question: Rinpoche, I have a question about chittamatra and the eighth consciousness. I'm wondering about how we take in new information. I'll use the example of coming to the teachings. If there is no "out there," and all experience is mind, my belief that I got on a plane and I came here and I heard teachings that I had not heard before is inaccurate. These were latencies in the eighth consciousness that emerged. I'm wondering how we then take in new information?

Rinpoche: The mind only school asserts that everything we experience is the display of habit, but the habits or imprints are of two types: those that are of the nature of bewilderment, and those that are counteractive to bewilderment. Those that are counteractive to bewilderment, that are imprints that are not of the nature of ignorance—it is hard even to call them imprints—they are the emergence of qualities of buddha nature, which qualities and which nature are held to be intrinsic to all beings. What this means is that buddha nature, which is the potential for awakening, is also the potential for all manner of virtues and qualities, because the root of these qualities is already present within us. Buddha nature is obscured by ignorance, causing us to experience in the bewildered way that we do. Under the power of ignorance we experience all sorts of things—places, and things, and so forth. In a situation where you appear to be acquiring wholly new information that is counteractive to ignorance—for example, like learning dharma or something like that—it is held that this is the awakening of buddha nature, and therefore the partial display of its qualities, which you experience as the acquisition of new information.

Same questioner: How does that acquisition of new information relate to the consciousnesses?

Rinpoche: Well, this plants new habits, further imprints, and reinforces the potential for awakening as well. Many people say to me that they are disappointed with the result of dharma practice, because they expect an immediate and dramatic change of some kind. Their attitude is one of two: If I have not attained awakening in a few years, then I have been wasting my time. If it is going to work, it should work immediately or, if it does not, then it is not working at all. I think that this expectation comes from your educational system. [laughter] You go to college and within three or four years, one hopes, you get a degree, and, if you do not, you have failed. It somehow did not work. So you have an attitude of either pass or fail. This means that you expect buddhahood to be imminent and, if it does not happen right away, you feel that it is just not working. It is important to understand, however, the context in which dharma practice occurs and how it affects you. If someone practices a tremendous amount and does change very quickly, of course, that is fantastic. But even if you practice only a little bit, everything that you do establishes and reinforces habitual imprints in your mind. Those habitual imprints are never lost. Therefore, there is no way that dharma practice can ever be a failure, because, however little of it you do and however little you feel that you have changed, you have established some kinds of habits that will continue to develop on their own through time just as a seed in a fertile environment will produce a sprout whether you observe its doing so or not. Therefore, even people who think that they have not achieved much through dharma practice are, in my opinion, very fortunate.

Time's up! [laughter]

[Rinpoche and students dedicate the merit.]

12 POINTING OUT THAT EMPTINESS IS SPONTANEOUS PRESENCE

POINTING OUT THE MIND within appearances has four parts: pointing out that appearances are mind, that mind is emptiness, that emptiness is spontaneous presence, and that spontaneous presence is self-liberation. Yesterday we completed the first two—pointing out that appearances are mind and that mind is emptiness. Today we are going to begin with the third, pointing out that emptiness is spontaneous presence.

First, it has been established that appearances are mind and then that mind lacks true existence, that its nature is emptiness. It is possible, however, that you might understand this emptiness or lack of true existence of the mind as nothingness, or that in the experience of meditation practice, when you look at the mind, you might experience some kind of nothing or nothingness. According to our text, if that is the case, your understanding is partial understanding and, if that is your experience, it is partial experience. Therefore, it is not regarded as genuine. In order to remove that potential for misunderstanding or partial understanding, what is presented next is pointing out that emptiness is spontaneous presence.

Talking about appearances, it was said by the Buddha, "Form is emptiness." One of the implications of this is that all of the things that we see— mountains, walls, buildings, and so forth—lack true, substantial existence, and that they lack true, substantial existence even on the level of truly existent subtle particles. But when it says that they are empty, aside from meaning that they are empty of existence, it is not saying that they are nothing. It is not saying that they are nothingness, nothing whatever, absolutely nothing. Therefore, in the *Heart Sutra* it continues, "Emptiness is form. Form is no other than emptiness. Emptiness is nothing other than form." Now, normally, if we were to think about this from an ordinary point of view, we would regard emptiness and form as contradictory. If something is empty, it is not there, and, therefore, is not a form. If something possesses form or is a form, it is something, and, therefore, is not empty. But this is not how things are. It is said, "There is no single thing anywhere that is not interdependent;

therefore, there is no single thing anywhere that is not empty." What is meant by emptiness is interdependence, and interdependence is also the appearance of things. Therefore, since emptiness and appearance are interdependent, emptiness and appearance are not contradictory in the way we normally regard them to be. For example, when you are asleep and dreaming, all of the things that you dream of—the houses and people and so on—do not exist. You are not actually in those houses; you are asleep at home in bed. Nevertheless, they do appear to you; there is a mere appearance of those things to the dreamer. Like that, the appearance of something, and its nonexistence, are not contradictory.

That was about appearances. Now, about mind, we have to consider the cognitive lucidity of mind. When you look at your mind, you initially look to see if it has any shape. Eventually you discover that the mind has no shape. You look to see if the mind has any color, and you discover that it has no color. You look to see if it has any other substantial or material characteristic, and you find that it does not. You look to see if it has a specific location within or outside the body, and you cannot find it. At some point you start to wonder, maybe I am not finding this because I do not know how to look. But that is not the case. It is not the case that you do not find any shape or color or substantial characteristic or location for the mind because you do not know how to look. Nor is it the case that you do not find these characteristics because, although the mind possesses them, they are too subtle to find. Nor is it the case that you do not find them because the mind is somehow too clear, too transparent, to be seen in this way. The reason that you do not find these things is that the very nature of the mind is emptiness. However, as in the case of appearances, emptiness here does not mean nothingness. The mind is empty, but it is not dead; it is not incapable of experience. It is not static or devoid of cognition. The mind can and does experience, can and does know. The mind's capacity to experience and to know is what we call its cognitive lucidity. Therefore, not only is the mind empty, but it is also lucid. However, if you then attempted to track down the mind's cognitive lucidity, find where it is, where it is seated, you would not find it. For example, when you look at the mind within the occurrence of thought, and so forth, you find that that cognitive lucidity itself is empty. You find this because the mind's cognitive lucidity is not separate from, is nothing other than, the mind's emptiness—just as the mind's emptiness is not apart from or separate from the mind's cognitive lucidity. There is no emptiness in the mind other than that cognitive lucidity. And there is no cognitive lucidity in the mind other than that emptiness. Now, this is very hard to relate to when we think about it, because normally we see these two characteristics as contradictory. We imagine that, if the mind is cognitive lucidity, it cannot be emptiness, and if the mind is emptiness, it cannot be cognitive lucidity. This is not a contradiction. When you look at the mind, while you find nothing, the cognitive lucidity of the mind remains continuous and functioning. The unity of cognitive lucidity and emptiness, which is our mind, is what is called the unity of awareness and emptiness, or the unity of lucidity and emptiness. Therefore, while the mind is lucid, it is empty; and while it is empty, it is lucid.

The importance of mentioning this is that you might otherwise wonder if meditation on mahamudra, meditation on the nature of mind, will cause you to become stupid and vacuous. You might wonder if somehow the only thing that maintains the lucidity of experience is fixation.[43] That is not the case. The cultivation of prajna or discernment involves three stages: the prajna of hearing, the prajna of thinking, and the prajna of meditation or meditating. The first two, the prajnas of hearing and thinking, are supposed to be developed prior to developing authentic experience and realization. The third one, the prajna of meditation, is the cultivation of that experience and realization. The term "prajna" implies particularly clear cognition or particularly clear knowledge—"pra" being an intensifier. Nevertheless, there is a further development of prajna, in which prajna is refined into wisdom or jnana. "Jnana" has the connotation of something that is stable and all-pervasive, something that is not cultivated, but discovered. You will remember several days ago I spoke of the shunyata mantra, which begins, OM SHUNYATA JNANA, and so on. The shunyata spoken of in the mantra is the emptiness, for example, of the mind, which is like an expanse. The wisdom or jnana of which the mantra speaks is that wisdom which is the mind's very cognitive lucidity, which is inseparable from that expanse. Because the mind is cognitive lucidity that is inseparable from emptiness, when you rest in that nature, you will not become stupid or vacuous. In other words, as you rest in the mind's nature, the wisdom increases and all of the qualities of wisdom increase. Therefore, the wisdom of a bodhisattva is far greater than the wisdom of an ordinary being. And the wisdom of a buddha is far greater than the wisdom of a bodhisattva. For example, when someone achieves buddhahood, they are said to possess two types of wisdom: the wisdom that knows what there is, which is the full knowledge of relative truth, and the wisdom that knows how things are, which is the full knowledge of absolute truth. You can also describe the wisdom of a buddha as the five wisdoms, and so forth. In any case, resting in the mind's nature leads to vast wisdom. All of that vast wisdom comes from the realization or seeing of dharmata, the essence of reality, which itself is realized, according to the tradition of practical instruction, within one's own mind—through looking at and recognizing one's mind's nature.

This nature of the mind at which we are looking, and that we come to recognize and realize, is not something new. It is not created by the practice. The nature in itself is not changed by the practice. It has always been there. The only change that has occurred or is occurring is that this nature has been introduced to you; it has been pointed out. And through that and through the instruction and through the blessings of the root and lineage gurus you come to recognize and realize it. Nevertheless, this nature is exactly the same nature that is spoken of in the sutras as sugatagarbha or buddha nature. In the sutras it is spoken of as a potential, like a seed that can be cultivated into the full state of awakening. If we look at the term "sugatagarbha," "su" means bliss. The bliss here is the bliss or supreme well-being that is beyond samsara and nirvana,[44] and it is that which is achieved when this nature is fully recognized. "Gata" means gone. So, one who has gone to bliss is a synonym for a buddha. But it is not the case that they have gone, and we cannot go. We too can go, or come to realize this, because we have this same potential. It is always there. It is our basic being, and, therefore, it is called "garbha."

From the point of view of mahamudra, we describe sugatagarbha as awareness/emptiness or the unity of awareness and emptiness, as lucidity/emptiness or the unity of lucidity and emptiness, and as bliss/emptiness or the unity of bliss and emptiness. This is significant, because we may wonder if progress in mahamudra meditation will lead to the diminishing of the intensity of experience, if it will lead to the cessation of all experience—to some kind of state of neutrality or vacuity. It does not. It leads to the realization of bliss/emptiness.

Among the sutras, the prajnaparamita sutras of the second dharmachakra primarily present emptiness. The last teachings of the Buddha, the third and final turning of the dharmachakra, emphasized buddha nature. These teachings on buddha nature were further expounded on and explained in the five treatises of Maitreya, among which the most extraordinary is the *Uttaratantra Shastra*. Central to the *Uttaratantra Shastra* is an explanation of the presence of buddha nature within us which uses nine different analogies to point out how it is present. One of these analogies is the analogy of gold concealed below the ground. The analogy in detail is as follows: Imagine that somehow a large lump of gold falls into the ground. It is subsequently further concealed by a landfill made of all sorts of garbage. The gold itself is utterly unaffected by this. It remains gold, just as it was, but it is not available to anyone directly. It does not fulfill its function as gold. Eventually a poor person builds a primitive shack on top of this garbage landfill. Directly underneath where he sleeps every night is this huge chunk of gold. So he has no need whatsoever to remain impoverished, but he does not know this, and therefore he suffers considerably from poverty. Someone who has extrasensory perception comes walking along, sees the shack and the terrible poverty of the person who lives in it, feels very bad for him, and also sees the gold that is right under his house. So he tells the person, "You do not need to be poor. You have a huge chunk of gold right under where you sleep every night." The poor person believes him, moves his mattress and starts digging, and sooner or later he finds that huge piece of gold. In the same way, each of us has buddha nature, dharmata, within us. But it is covered by our obscurations: the cognitive obscurations and the afflictive obscurations.

Since we regard ourselves to be our obscurations, we are always looking outside ourselves; we are always looking away from our own buddha nature. The primary function, the primary deed of the Buddha and his followers, is to tell us to look within, to tell us that within our bewildered minds is innate wisdom, there to be discovered if we look. Through the blessing of this we need not suffer further the bewilderment of samsara, which is like the poverty of the person in the shack.

That is what is presented in the *Uttaratantra Shastra.* In the sutras, buddha nature is presented as an object of inferential valid cognition, whereas in mahamudra this same buddha nature is presented as an object of direct valid cognition. Aside from that, the understanding of buddha nature is very similar. Therefore, Lord Gampopa said that the mahamudra practice of our lineage depends upon the five treatises of Maitreya. So that is pointing out emptiness to be spontaneous presence, and I am going to stop there for this morning and continue with the reading transmission.

[Rinpoche continues with the reading transmission.]

[Rinpoche and students dedicate the merit.]

13 POINTING OUT THAT SPONTANEOUS PRESENCE IS SELF-LIBERATION

NOW WE COME to the fourth part of pointing out the mind within appearances, which is pointing out that spontaneous presence is self-liberation. First we meditate on appearances as mind, and then on mind as emptiness. Then, in order to ensure the recognition that emptiness, which is the nature of the mind, is not nothingness and absolutely nothing like space, emptiness is presented as being spontaneous presence. In the context of appearances, this means that emptiness is the potential for the appearance of relative truths,[45] and that it is the unity of appearance and emptiness. In the context of the mind itself, the mind's emptiness is the unity of cognitive lucidity and emptiness, the unity of awareness and emptiness, and the unity of great bliss and emptiness. The nature of emptiness is at the same time great bliss and, therefore, when it is fully realized, great bliss is achieved. In order to point all of this out, emptiness is pointed out as spontaneous presence. Therefore, spontaneous presence itself is the basis for liberation.

Liberation here is liberation from suffering, the end of suffering, which is brought about through liberation from the cause of suffering, the kleshas. It is also liberation from the most subtle obscurations, the cognitive obscurations. What is pointed out here is that this liberation is not produced by effort. Those things that are to be abandoned in order to attain liberation have no existence. Therefore, liberation happens of its own nature, and is therefore called self-liberation.

The reason why spontaneous presence is self-liberated starts with the following: In samsara we experience a great variety of different kinds of suffering, and there are many different kleshas that are present in the minds of beings as causes and conditions for this suffering. But all of these things are empty. For example, in the practice called "looking at the mind within the occurrence of thought," when you look at the three poisons—attachment, aversion, and apathy—or when you look at the states of delight and misery, while normally we are overpowered by these states of mind and come under their control, when you actually look at them, you see that their nature is emptiness.

Simply in having seen that, we are very fortunate. If kleshas really existed, if they had true and solid existence, it would require effort to abandon them. But once you see their emptiness, once you see that they are empty, they will gradually disappear.

I say "gradually," because simply seeing the emptiness of one particular klesha on one occasion does not prevent the reoccurrence of kleshas. When you practice tranquility meditation, one of the effects is that your kleshas are weakened, but, as you will remember, aside from weakening them, the practice of tranquility does not eradicate them. But when you practice insight meditation, you actually see their nonexistence. Through seeing the nonexistence of a klesha, it is conquered, it is completely pacified. That particular klesha at that moment is pacified and conquered, but that does not prevent a reoccurrence. The reason why simply seeing the emptiness of a klesha once does not prevent its reoccurrence is that we have a strong habit of entertaining kleshas, which we have accumulated throughout beginningless time. For example, you look at your mind and you observe the emptiness of a thought or klesha that is present within it. Then you arise from that meditation and you no longer observe the emptiness of thoughts and kleshas. In other words, simply observing the emptiness of kleshas on one occasion is not the end of the path.

There will also be fluctuations in your experience, which means that sometimes you will have a heightened awareness of the emptiness of kleshas, and it will be easy to observe that emptiness directly; and sometimes your awareness of emptiness will seem somehow dull or diminished, and it will not serve to enable you to see the emptiness of your kleshas. As long as the habit of indulging kleshas has not been eradicated, there will continue to be the need actually to observe their emptiness again and again.

The distinction between what happens when you see the emptiness of a klesha and what happens when you have actually fully eradicated all kleshas forever is, in the context of the graduated path, a distinction between the wisdom of the path of seeing and the wisdom of the path of meditation or cultivation.[46] Although someone has seen dharmata, has directly experienced the nature of mind, this insight has to be further cultivated. In the same way, on the path of mahamudra, if having seen the emptiness of kleshas in experience once, you do not continue to cultivate that insight and you just abandon it, this will not have any effect on the rest of your kleshas. So there is a great deal of difference between what is abandoned simply through being seen once or a few times, and what has to be abandoned through the path of cultivation. Therefore it has been said by many mahasiddhas, "Our bad habits are like the tendency of a scroll that has been kept rolled up to roll itself back up every time we try to unroll it." The insight into the nature of one klesha is not the end of the path.

Therefore, even practitioners who have realized the nature of mind must continue practicing meditation. And it need not be said that practitioners who have not realized the nature of mind must also continue practicing. In short, the actual practice of meditation is very important. As was said by Jamgön Kongtrül Lodrö Thayé in *The Essence of Generation and Completion*, "The achievement of the final fruition depends upon continuous diligent application. This in turn must be carried out throughout both meditation and post-meditation, through the application of both mindfulness and alertness."

As for what the result of practice is, it has been said by many teachers, "The sign of having heard the dharma is to be peaceful and subdued. The sign of having meditated is to have no kleshas." It is said that you can tell whether or not you have genuinely heard the teachings and understood their point by whether or not you are tame and peaceful in your conduct. And you can tell whether or not your meditation is effective by whether or not your kleshas are diminishing. Ideally, someone should finally have no kleshas whatsoever. But even on the way to that klesha-free state, your kleshas and thoughts should diminish. Therefore, I think that it is of far greater importance than the experience of dramatic instantaneous pointing out that people be taught mahamudra as a full system of instruction that they can implement on their own gradually through diligent application using either one of the three texts by the Ninth Gyalwang Karmapa—*The Ocean of Definitive Meaning, Dispelling the Darkness of Ignorance,* or *Pointing Out the Dharmakaya*—or one of the texts by Dakpo Tashi Namgyal—either *Moonbeams of Mahamudra* or *The Clarification of the Natural State*.

In short, I think it is of far more importance that people receive this kind of complete and systematic instruction so that they can gradually develop experience on their own, than that some kind of dramatic pointing-out procedure be done. Of course, it is possible to give dramatic pointing-out instruction, and when you do so, some people do recognize their mind's nature. But, if I may say so, I question the stability and, therefore, ultimately the value of that. It certainly is a dramatic experience for those people who achieve it, but I see no evidence of their kleshas diminishing as a result. And furthermore, they then carry away with them the arrogance of the thought, "I have seen my mind's nature." I think it is of far greater importance actually to practice meditation slowly and surely and make all possible use of the resources which this book in particular gives you. It is after all a big book and contains within it much instruction, much guidance, and a lot of questions that can help you to question and therefore refine your own experience. When you make use of this book in applying it to your own practice, do not do so in a vague or casual way; do not look at a description of experience and think, "Well, that must be what I am seeing—after all that is what it says in the book." Continue with each phase of the practice until you actually have definite experience that you are sure of. Remember, especially, that what you are looking at and what you are looking for is just the nature of your own mind. It is therefore not far away from you. It is not something that you have to search for in the manner of a hunter pursuing a deer through a dense forest. It is right with you. Therefore, in itself it is not really difficult to recognize.

So, we must practice meditation, and through meditation we have to generate real experience of our own mind. For this purpose, therefore, precise and complete instruction is very valuable. We have available to us the advice of so many great teachers who preceded us in the same path. All of these beings are embodied in and contained in the text that we are studying.

However, I do not want to give you the impression that, while we need to practice mahamudra, there is no need for any other kind of practice at all, because that is not true either. The purpose of practicing mahamudra is first to develop prajna and finally to discover jnana or wisdom, and we must do anything we need to do to develop these qualities. Now, one issue is that there are times when you simply cannot rest in the nature of your mind, [and therefore it is virtually impossible to practice mahamudra.] Therefore, it is good to understand that there are many supplementary practices that will facilitate, enhance, and therefore make easier, the practice of mahamudra. For example, the preliminary practices or ngöndro are valuable for mahamudra practice, because they increase renunciation and devotion. Also, the generation stage practices connected with any yidam—and it does not matter which yidam it is—help a great deal. When you practice the generation stage you are working with your mind in the context of that iconography. This is very helpful in the cultivation of both tranquility and insight. Furthermore, in the context of such practices, when you perform the invitation liturgy, and so on, the devotion that you generate can change your attitude of mind, such that it can bring genuine experience.

Another issue is that we are especially plagued by our perception of impurity. Characteristic of samsara is that we see everything as impure. We need to transform our perception of impurity into the perception of purity. But we cannot do so as long as we continue to reinforce this perception of impurity. Therefore, in order to remedy that fault, we visualize a yidam or deity. Basically we do this in two ways: One way is called self-generation, in which you visualize yourself as the deity; the other way is called front visualization, in which you visualize the deity in front of you.

The purpose of self-generation, visualizing yourself as a yidam deity, is to gradually reveal buddha nature. It is effective because yidams are all manifestations of the buddha nature or sugatagarbha, the innate potential of awakening that we all have. By visualizing yourself, not in your ordinary form or body, but in the pure form of a yidam, you gradually reveal that nature. This is a special technique of the vajrayana, as is front visualization.

The reason for front generation, front visualization is that, if you only did self-visualization and not also front visualization, you might think that the yidam embodied only your buddha nature, that there was no possibility of any help from outside. That is simply not true; there are innumerable buddhas and bodhisattvas, and having achieved awakening, they actually can see us, although we cannot see them. When you visualize a yidam in front of you, you are considering that to be the presence of all buddhas and bodhisattvas in the form of that particular yidam. And when you cultivate devotion in that way for that yidam, then you receive the blessings and the assistance of all those buddhas and bodhisattvas.

Many yidam practices have a third type of visualization, called vase generation, in which you visualize all buddhas and bodhisattvas again in the form of that particular yidam or deity as present in the vase which will subsequently be used in self-empowerment. Finally, at a particular stage in the generation stage practice, they dissolve into and become indivisible from the water in the vase, which is then used to confer the empowerment. This is not pretending that one thing is something else, because the empowerment confers the blessing of that deity; therefore, it is in fact meaningful to visualize that deity as present within the receptacle or implement of empowerment.

Another especially important supplementary practice for mahamudra practitioners is guru yoga. Guru yoga may be meditation on one's root guru or may be meditation on any guru of the lineage. It is necessary to make this clear, because, while some people have unchanging faith in their root guru, other people do not. So, if you find that you lack that type of inspiration of unchanging faith in your root guru, then study the lives of the gurus of the lineage and supplicate one or more of them, and their blessings will enter into you.

When we use the word blessing, do not expect this necessarily to be something dramatic and overwhelming. Blessing is not necessarily going to make you shake and quake. The receipt of blessing actually is indicated when your mind starts to change. Whereas before you may not have had stable faith in the guru, in the teachings, and so forth, your faith becomes stable; whereas before you lacked devotion for practice, you now start to have it; whereas before your kleshas were uncontrollable, they start to diminish; whereas before you were unable to see anything wrong whatsoever with obsessive involvement in mundane activities, you start to detect that they are pointless. These are all indications of receiving blessing.

In order to induce the receipt of blessing, you can either use the sadhana of a yidam or the practice of guru yoga. Other supplementary practices include the *lo jong* teachings in general[47] and especially the practice of *tonglen*,[48] and other things that are less formal—for example, letting go of your greedy and obsessive attachment to things; starting to practice useful acts of generosity, such as giving to those in actual need, and in that way, actually setting about the proper practice of the six perfections of generosity, moral discipline, patience, exertion or diligence, meditation, and prajna, and so on. It is not absolutely necessary to attempt to imitate the inconceivable deeds of great bodhisattvas. Nevertheless, it is important to open your mind to the possibility of doing so. If you can actually do so, of course, that is fine, too. And finally, another supplementary practice that should be mentioned is the dedication of virtue to the awakening of all beings.

All of these supplementary practices exist for one reason. They exist in order to assist the achievement of mahamudra realization. Therefore, it was said by Shantideva, "All of these branches were taught by the Sage for the sake of prajna." In other words, the first five perfections, from generosity up to and including meditation, were taught by the Buddha as methods leading to the achievement of the sixth, prajna. The point of all of these supplementary practices is the realization of mahamudra. Since they are conducive to and supportive of gaining that realization, they are by no means unimportant.

There is something else to which we must always pay attention, and that is what the Buddha referred to as the ten virtuous and ten unvirtuous actions. It is important, as much as one can, to avoid the ten unvirtuous actions and to engage in the ten virtuous actions. Sometimes you can do so perfectly and completely—you can avoid everything that is unvirtuous and you can practice a great deal that is virtuous. And sometimes you cannot. But it is important always to keep in mind the direction in which you are moving; the goal that you are seeking in your conduct is to avoid completely that which is harmful and to do that which is beneficial. Sometimes you are forced to do something that is negative, whether because of your previous karma or immediate conditions. Through maintaining mindfulness, alertness, and watchfulness, not just in meditation, but also in post-meditation, try to cultivate virtue and to avoid that which is unvirtuous. This is for your own benefit, because it is very hard to realize mahamudra in the midst of an unvirtuous life. Therefore, please practice mindfulness and alertness in post-meditation as well.

I am going to stop here for this afternoon, and now we will meditate a little bit.

[Rinpoche meditates with students.]

[Rinpoche and students dedicate the merit.]

14 Bringing Gradual
Improvement to the Practice

Yesterday I explained how spontaneous presence is pointed out as self-liberation. That is the forty-fifth and last practice session in our text. The rest of the book from then on is all teaching sessions. There are no additional practice sessions. Within the same section of the book there are several quotations from sutras, tantras, and the words of great gurus of the past. And then the section of the text that is the main practice is concluded and we come to the final section of the text, which is the conclusion. Much of the conclusion is concerned with the enhancement of the practice, with how to bring about gradual improvement. Enhancement is explained in detail, all in teaching sessions; no separate practice sessions are presented.

The first section of the conclusion is the dispelling of impediments. This is divided into six points. The most important of these are places of loss and places of deviation. There are four places of loss and one place of deviation described, making a total of five. The four places of loss are explained in the sixty-fifth, sixty-sixth, sixty-seventh, and sixty-eighth teaching sessions. What is meant by a place of loss is something that causes you to take entirely the wrong approach or entirely the wrong path, to mistake the path fundamentally.

Although there are four of these spoken of in our text, most prevalent are two. One is less serious, but still a problem, and the other one is most serious, and most definitely a problem. The one that is less serious but still a problem is to confuse experience and understanding, to develop through inferential reasoning an understanding of something and to mistake that understanding for actual direct experience. This type of confusion or place of loss is a problem because it prevents progress. Obviously, if one attempts to cultivate inferential understanding as the basis of one's practice, one will not get anywhere. But it is not dangerous in any other way.

The second place of loss is truly dangerous, and this is to develop an intellectual view of emptiness that makes you nihilistic—to have some understanding or some experience of emptiness and then mistakenly to conclude, based on that understanding or experience, that nothing matters, that there is no benefit to virtue because it is empty, and that there is nothing problematic about wrongdoing because it is empty. This is called carrying emptiness around in your mouth. This is the very worst place of loss and the very worst misunderstanding that can occur. These two are the major places of loss. The first needs to be avoided for progress to occur, but it is, aside from that, not dangerous. The second is extremely dangerous.

Both of these places of loss are somewhat easy to recognize and, therefore, they are easy to abandon or relinquish. As long as you continue to cultivate mindfulness, alertness, and watchfulness, there should be no problem in recognizing them if they start to afflict you. And having recognized them, it should not be too difficult to abandon them. Again, of these two, the one that is the greatest danger is the view of nothingness or nihilism—the thought that nothing matters.

In the sixty-ninth teaching session the places of deviation are presented. The difference between places of loss and places of deviation is that, whereas a place of loss takes you on the wrong path altogether, a place of deviation causes you to be somewhat sidetracked. Another way to distinguish between them is that, generally speaking, places of loss arise because of how you are thinking, and places of deviation can arise based on actual meditation experience on which you fixate. As you practice, various experiences can arise: experiences of intense well-being or bliss; experiences of both cognitive and sensory lucidity; and experiences of no-thought, experiences of nonconceptuality. Regardless of what arises, if you attach an independent value to the experience, and in that way become attached to the repetition or perpetuation of the experience, that will impede your progress. Whatever arises, whatever the experience is, and whether or not any special experience arises at all, it is essential to have no attachment to what arises and no craving for its rearising. If extraordinary experiences occur for you, simply continue your practice without being led astray by them. If extraordinary experiences do not arise for you, simply continue your practice without craving their arising.

Mainly what we are seeking in the practice of meditation is stability and lucidity. Experiences, including visions, are not that important. This needs to be said, because otherwise you might think that visions, such as different things you see when you meditate, are either special in some way or a sign of some danger. For example, if you look at the life of Lord Gampopa, when he was practicing meditation under the guidance of Jetsun Milarepa, he started to experience a lot of different visions and he naturally assumed that these were of some significance. So, he went into Milarepa's presence and reported the visions that he had been seeing. Milarepa responded by saying,

"Well, there is nothing wrong, but this is nothing special either. Just continue practicing." Milarepa said that seeing visions is like someone who squeezes their eyes, presses on their eyes and looks at the moon and sees two moons. There could be two different reactions to this. One person would look and see two moons and think that he or she was special. "Everyone else sees just one moon. I see two." Another person would look at the sky and see two moons and think that they were losing their mind. "Everyone else sees one moon. I see two." In fact, if you see visions and various sorts of things there is nothing wrong. You are not losing your mind. But it does not mean that you are anything special either. You see things simply because you are working with your mind directly. Therefore, the mind is somehow stimulated and can produce these visions. But they are not dangerous. They are not going to cause you to lose your mind. Since meditation for us is to remain looking at the mind's nature, do not react with fear or pride to any visions that occur.

What is of primary importance, of course, is that we continue to cultivate the samadhi of mahamudra. Also pointed out in this section of the text is the importance that this cultivation not become partial. In other words, it is important not to cultivate an experience of emptiness that is devoid of compassion, or to cultivate compassion in the absence of the experience of emptiness. Either one will be incomplete. In practice this means that, while we continue to meditate on the mind's nature, it is important to continue to cultivate the lo jong training and the practice of tonglen. Compassion and the cultivation of compassion will cause progress in your realization of emptiness, and the realization of emptiness will naturally increase your compassion. The development of compassion in this context, however, has to be free, as much as possible, of dualism. About this it was said by the Third Gyalwang Karmapa, Rangjung Dorge, "Through this meditation, intolerable[49] compassion for beings will arise spontaneously. At the very moment that that love arises or appears, its emptiness of nature will be directly or nakedly evident. May I, therefore, cultivate throughout the day and the night this supreme path, which in this unity is beyond deviation."[50] Through the force of meditation on the mind's nature, compassion will arise spontaneously. The arising of compassion will enhance the recognition of mind's nature.

The second thing that is mentioned in this section of the text is the relationship between two aspects of practice: upaya (method) and prajna (discernment). In this context the development of prajna primarily refers to the cultivation of the samadhi of mahamudra. The practice of method or upaya primarily refers to the gathering of the accumulations, specifically to the accumulation of merit. If someone takes only method as their practice, gathering the accumulations without any cultivation of prajna, then their prac-

tice strays into the extreme of permanence, because, for it ultimately to lead
to wisdom, merit and the accumulation of merit must be sealed by the
absence of reification of the three aspects of that accumulation.[51]

On the other hand, if we utterly ignore the accumulation of merit, then
our cultivation of prajna can sometimes be weakened. In this case, we cannot perfect the power of prajna because there is not the necessary energy to
do so. In such cases, the application of method, including the gathering of
the accumulation of merit, can bring a great increase to the force of the prajna that one has cultivated through meditation. In that way, method is caused
to increase—as in the increased accumulation of merit through the application of greater prajna—and prajna will increase through the application of
method. Here, what is referred to as method or upaya is in general the first
five of the six perfections (paramitas), not including discernment or prajna—
generosity, patience, discipline, exertion, and meditation—and also specific
methods, such as the practice of guru yoga, the practice of meditation on
yidams, and so forth, all of which are useful in bringing progress in mahamudra practice.

The third point connected with enhancement is the relationship between
tranquility and insight. It has been stated that if we only practice tranquility
without developing any practice of insight, we will not achieve the qualities
of abandonment and realization.[52] Therefore, we clearly need the practice of
insight.

However, if, on the other hand, we underemphasize the practice of tranquility and only practice insight in isolation from tranquility, because any
insight gained under such conditions will be unstable, we will be unable to
bring the practice of insight to perfection. Therefore, as was the case with
compassion and emptiness, and method and prajna, here, tranquility and
insight reinforce and bring progress to one another. Tranquility enhances
one's progress in developing insight, because it brings stability to it, and
insight enhances one's progress in developing tranquility, because it brings
lucidity to it. In practice this means that one primarily practices insight, but
one continues to cultivate within that samadhi of insight the stability that was
gained through the preceding practice of tranquility.

In that way, although we call our practice insight, in fact, it is the unity or
integration of tranquility and insight. If at any point your cultivation of
insight becomes unstable, if your mind becomes too conceptual because of
the process of investigation, you can always return to the specific tranquility
practices and apply them as needed to regain the necessary stability. So in that
way, through the integration of compassion and emptiness, the integration

of method and discernment, and the integration of tranquility and insight, progress will be ensured.

That is how to practice mahamudra according to *The Ocean of Definitive Meaning*. When you study this book on your own, carefully and gradually, as I hope you will, you will observe that it is very clear. It gives very precise practical instructions for every stage of the entire path—from the stage of an absolute beginner to the stage of greater no-meditaton. The book is utterly clear and utterly profound. Now you have to actually accomplish this path through practice. Therefore, at each stage of your practice, continue to consult the book. Consult the sections of the book that correspond to where you actually have reached in your practice and your experience. And carefully compare your experience of practice to what is presented at that point in the book, stage by stage. Do not let this comparison become too vague. Do not allow guess work or inference to interfere with authentic evaluation of your practice, based upon the prescription or instruction that you find in the book. This book exists through the great compassion of the gurus of our lineage. It is based on their direct experience, not upon dogma or upon theory of any kind. It is, therefore, not a general survey of the path. It is without any vagueness or mistake in its presentation of the path. Read it very carefully and use it assiduously to guide your practice. Because this book is devoted solely to direct and practical instruction, it is more a case of directly pointing things out about practice and about the mind than giving supportive arguments and explanations for why this is the case and why that is the case.

So, this book does not present a lot of logical arguments. You will not find many proofs of the various ideas that are presented here. There are two ways you can approach dharma: You can base your approach on faith, or you can base it on reasoning and logic. Most Western students follow reasoning or logic as opposed to simple faith, which is good. That may mean, however, that, while *The Ocean of Definitive Meaning* will definitely give enough material and instruction for your practice itself, you may still have questions about the background of the practice or about the reasons for certain things that are said that this book does not answer. If that does occur, I urge you to consult *Moonbeams of Mahamudra* (translated as *Mahamudra: The Quintessence of Mind and Meditation*)[53] by Dakpo Tashi Namgyal, because that book is also a source of practical guidance, but does give some of the theoretical background about which you may wish to know.

I am going to stop here and finish the reading transmission.

[Rinpoche finishes the reading transmission.]

[Rinpoche and students dedicate the merit:]

Unborn, eternal, self-arising dharmakaya
Arises as the miraculous kayas of form;
May the three secrets of the Karmapa be stable in the vajra nature
And may his limitless buddha activity spontaneously blaze.

Splendor of the Teachings, Venerable Karma Lodro, may you remain
*   steadfastly present.*
Your qualities of the glorious and excellent dharma increase to fill space.
May your lotus-feet always be stable,
And may your buddha activity of teaching and practice blaze in all
*   directions.*

By this merit, may all attain omniscience.
May it defeat the enemy, wrongdoing.
From the stormy waves of birth, old age, sickness, and death,
From the ocean of samsara may I free all beings.

NOTES

1 Published in 2001 by Nitartha *international* under the title *Mahamudra: The Ocean of Definitive Meaning*. For further information go to www.nitartha.org.

2 Tranquility meditation is commonly referred to by the Sanskrit word *shamatha* and by the Tibetan word *shinay*.

3 Insight meditation is commonly referred to by the Sanskrit word *vipashyana* and by the Tibetan word *lhaktong*.

4 The common preliminaries, which are common in the sense of being shared by all traditions of Buddhism, include the teachings on precious human birth, death and impermanence, karmic cause and effect, and the unsatisfactory or vicious nature of samsara. The uncommon preliminaries include going for refuge and engendering bodhicitta, using prostrations as a support; the purification practice of Vajrasattva; the gathering of the two accumulations of merit and wisdom through the practice of mandala offerings; and the receipt of the blessings of the lama's lineage of mahamudra through guru yoga. For a discussion of the third set of preliminaries, called particular or special preliminaries, see *Shenpen Ösel* 4, no. 3 (2000): 12-17.

5 The Six Dharmas of Naropa are six special yogic practices received by Naropa from Tilopa and subsequently passed down through the Kagyu lineages to the present day. They are the yogas of *chandali* (Sanskrit) or *tumo* (Tibetan), illusory body, dream, luminosity, ejection of consciousness, and the bardo.

6 See *Shenpen Ösel* 1, no. 2 (1997): 11-13 for Rinpoche's explanation of the seven dharmas of Vairochana.

7 See Kalu Rinpoche, *THE DHARMA That Illuminates All Beings Impartially Like the Light of the Sun and the Moon* (Albany: State University of New York Press, 1986), pp. 151-171 and 181-183 for a discussion and enumeration of the fifty-one samskaras or mental formations.

8 I.e., not through the practice of deity meditation, nor through the various associated completion stage practices such as the Six Dharmas of Naropa, the Six Dharmas of Niguma, or the Six Applications of Kalachakra, all of which involve various visualizations. For more on the creation and completion stages of tantric meditation practice, see *Shenpen Ösel* 5, no. 1 (2001).

9 Post-meditation refers to all time not spent in formal meditation.

10 The three prayers offered are, respectively, the Long Life Prayer for the Seventeenth Gyalwa Karmapa, Ögyen Trinley Dorje; the Long Life Prayer for Thrangu Rinpoche; and the Dedication of Merit Prayer.

11 It is visualized as a two dimensional square that has a bit of thickness in the third dimension, like the visualization of a thick square coin.

12 Blue for ignorance, confusion, apathy, and/or bewilderment; white for anger; and red for passion. The consequence of successfully visualizing these faces radiantly is to transform these kleshas, which are based on dualistic clinging and are impure in nature, into their wisdom aspects, which transcend dualistic clinging and are therefore pure in nature. The radiant blue face then represents the transformation of ignorance into the wisdom of dharmadhatu; the radiant white face then represents the transformation of anger into the mirror-like wisdom; and the radiant red face then represents the transformation of desire into the discriminating awareness wisdom. For further information about the fives wisdoms, see Thrangu Rinpoche's commentary on the symbolism of the five buddhas of the five buddha families in *Shenpen Ösel* 4, no. 2 (2000): 25-26.

13 The vajra-like samadhi occurs at the end of the tenth bhumi of bodhisattva attainment and signifies the attainment of the state of buddhahood.

14 *Chandali* and the breathing and physical exercises that go with it are very dangerous if not practiced in seclusion under the supervision of a qualified lama, with the proper motivation, and with proper preparation in meditation.

15 See *Shenpen Ösel* 1, no.2 (1997): 16-17 and *Shenpen Ösel* 3, no. 2 (1999): 3, 49.

16 In the experience of tranquility, the struggle against thoughts ceases through the recognition that if you simply leave the mind alone, thoughts are seen to dissolve of their own accord. It is also seen that struggling against thoughts only creates more thoughts, and since the bias of tranquility meditation is towards being without thoughts, one gives up the struggle against them and allows them to dissolve naturally. In the experience of mahamudra, on the other hand, once the mind's nature has truly been recognized, thoughts are directly experienced as being of the same essence as mind itself. Therefore, whether or not there are thoughts in the mind, the ultimate nature of the mind and of the mind's contents is in essence exactly the same. Therefore, the presence or absence of thoughts is irrelevant.

17 The distinction between mindfulness and alertness is important in Buddhism. The faculty of mind that determines to do something or not to do something and remembers that it has made such a determination is called mindfulness. The faculty of clear awareness that enables the mind to notice that in fact it is not doing what it had determined to do or is doing what it determined not to do is called alertness.

18 One is not to allow one's awareness to drift from seeing very clearly where you are and what you are doing and experiencing in the present. One is not to drift off into thoughts of the future at the expense of awareness of the present, nor to drift off into thoughts of the past at the expense of awareness of the present. But thoughts about the past and the future that are experienced in an awareness that they are current events happening in the present, that do not cause one to drift off into daydreams

about the past and the future, are perfectly all right, and one does not attempt to stop their arising or to alter them in any way.

19 For the complete prayer and Tai Situ Rinpoche's commentary on it, see *Shenpen Ösel* 2, no. 1 (1998).

20 Karma refers both to any action, good or bad, that is motivated by a mind under the influence of dualistic clinging—i.e., clinging to subject and object, good and bad, pleasant and unpleasant, etc.—and to the results of such actions.

21 The Sanskrit word *klesha* has had many translations—emotional affliction, conflicting emotion, emotional disturbance—and refers to any state of mind, whether we might regard it as being good or bad, that is under the power of dualistic fixation and thus serves as the motivation for the actions and results we refer to as karma. Therefore, kleshas are seen as a more fundamental cause of suffering than karma. In the hinayana teachings, the Buddha presents the belief in the existence of an individual self as the basis of the arising of kleshas, and presents meditations leading to the realization of the nonexistence of an individual self as the principal remedy to the arising of kleshas. As the Buddha continued to discuss the causes of suffering, his presentation came to include subtler causes. Principal among these are dualistic fixation—clinging to the existence of an individual self and fixation on the existence of that which is other to the self—and fundamental ignorance, the fundamental misperception of the nature of mind and the nature of reality. Thus, suffering arises from karma—including emotional reactivity and "karmic retribution"; karma arises from kleshas; kleshas arise from dualistic fixation; and dualistic fixation arises from the fundamental misperception of the nature of things, which includes the nature of mind and the nature of reality. As we shall see, the true and sustained recognition of the nature of mind and reality causes this concatenation of the causes of suffering to collapse like a house of cards. See *Shenpen Ösel* 3, no. 1 (1999): 3-31 for Kyabje Kalu Rinpoche's presentation of this topic.

22 *The Sutra of the Heart of Transcendent Knowledge*:

Thus have I heard.

Once the Blessed One was dwelling in Rajagriha at Vulture Peak mountain, together with a great gathering of the sangha of monastics and a great gathering of the sangha of bodhisattvas. At that time the Blessed One entered the samadhi that expresses the dharma called "profound illumination," and at the same time noble Avalokiteshvara, the bodhisattva mahasattva, while practicing the profound prajnaparamita, saw in this way: He saw the five skandhas to be empty of nature.

Then, through the power of the Buddha, venerable Shariputra said to noble Avalokiteshvara, the bodhisattva mahasattva, "How should a son or daughter of noble family train, who wishes to practice the profound prajnaparamita?"

Addressed in this way, noble Avalokiteshvara, the bodhisattva mahasattva, said to venerable Shariputra, "O Shariputra, a son or daughter of noble family who wishes to practice the profound prajnaparamita should see in this way: seeing the five skandhas to be empty of nature. Form is emptiness; emptiness also is form. Emptiness is no other than form; form is no other than emptiness. In the same way, feeling, perception, formation, and consciousness are emptiness. Thus,

Shariputra, all dharmas are emptiness. There are no characteristics. There is no birth and no cessation. There is no impurity and no purity. There is no decrease and no increase. Therefore, Shariputra, in emptiness, there is no form, no feeling, no perception, no formation, no consciousness; no eye, no ear, no nose, no tongue, no body, no mind; no appearance, no sound, no smell, no taste, no touch, no dharmas; no eye dhatu up to no mind dhatu, no dhatu of dharmas, no mind consciousness dhatu; no ignorance, no end of ignorance up to no old age and death, no end of old age and death; no suffering, no origin of suffering, no cessation of suffering, no path, no wisdom, no attainment, and no nonattainment. Therefore, Shariputra, since the bodhisattvas have no attainment, they abide by means of prajnaparamita. Since there is no obscuration of mind, there is no fear. They transcend falsity and attain complete nirvana. All the buddhas of the three times, by means of prajnaparamita, fully awaken to unsurpassable, true, complete enlightenment. Therefore, the great mantra of prajnaparamita, the mantra of great insight, the unsurpassed mantra, the unequaled mantra, the mantra that calms all suffering, should be known as truth, since there is no deception. The prajnaparamita mantra is said in this way:

OM GATE GATE PARAGATE PARASAMGATE BODHI SVAHA

Thus, Shariputra, the bodhisattva mahasattva should train in the profound prajnaparamita."

Then the Blessed One arose from that samadhi and praised noble Avalokiteshvara, the bodhisattva mahasattva, saying "Good, good, O son of noble family; thus it is, O son of noble family, thus it is. One should practice the profoundprajnaparamita just as you have taught and all the tathagatas will rejoice."

When the Blessed One had said this, venerable Shariputra and noble Avalokiteshvara, the bodhisattva mahasattva, that whole assembly and the world with its gods, humans, asuras, and gandharvas rejoiced and praised the words of the Blessed One.

English translation by the Nalanda Translation Committee,
as slightly amended by Shenpen Ösel.

23 There are many different forms of prajna. First there is worldly prajna, which would include, from the standpoint of relative truth, any unconfused knowledge about the workings of the world that we might study in colleges and universities. Then there is spiritual prajna, which includes what we would call unconfused knowledge of spiritual matters and transcendental insight on the one hand, and jnana, which is translated variously as original wisdom or primordial awareness, and sometimes just as wisdom, on the other.

24 For a short description of the generation and completion stages of vajrayana meditation, see Thrangu Rinpoche's teaching on the tantric path of mahamudra in *Shenpen Ösel* 2, no. 2 (1998): 50-58. For a more extensive treatment, see Thrangu Rinpoche's commentary on Jamgön Kongtrül's text *Creation and Completion* in *Shenpen Ösel* 5, no. 1 (2001): 4-61.

25 The syllable OM embodies the blessings of the forms of all the buddhas and bodhisattvas of the three times and ten directions, including the blessings of body of all

lamas, yidams, dakas, dakinis, and dharma protectors, and, thus, of the yidam being practiced.

26 Empty of any inherent, substantial, indivisible, separate, and unchanging existence.

27 I.e., the self that we and others believe exists and that we project onto that which does not exist, thereby providing the basis for perceiving the self as existent.

28 For further discussion of these two topics, including the many proofs of both Nagarjuna, Chandrakirti, and Asanga, see the teachings of Khenpo Tsultrim Gyamtso Rinpoche in *Shenpen Ösel* 2, no. 2 (1998); 3, no. 2 (1999); and 5, nos. 2-3 (2001). Also see Khenchen Thrangu Rinpoche's *Open Door to Emptiness* and Khenpo Tsultrim Gyamtso Rinpoche's *Progressive Stages of Meditation on Emptiness* (both available through Namo Buddha Publications: cjohnson@ix.netcom.com); Arya Maitreya's *The Changeless Nature* (*The Mahayana Uttaratantra Shastra*) translated by Ken and Katia Holmes, with extensive notes provided through consultation with both Thrangu Rinpoche and Khenpo Tsultrim Gyamtso Rinpoche (available at www.samyelingshop.com); and Arya Maitreya's *Buddha Nature* (*The Mahayana Uttaratantra Shastra*), with Jamgön Kongtrül Lodrö Thaye's commentary *The Unassailable Lion's Roar* and Khenpo Tsultrim Gyamtso Rinpoche's commentary on Jamgön Kongtrül's commentary (available at www.snowlionpub.com).

29 Nor will it by itself lead to liberation.

30 Any practice of the path of method—including *ngöndro*, any form of guru yoga or yidam or protector practice, *chandali*, etc.—will help to dispel torpor. When practicing front visualizations, focusing on the upper part of the visualization helps to dispel torpor. Splashing cold water in one's face, taking cold showers, running around the block, reducing the temperature in the room, opening the windows, taking off some clothing, tightening up one's posture—all will help to dispel torpor.

31 Concentrating on the lower parts of either a self visualization or a front visualization, relaxing one's posture and making oneself comfortable, and increasing the warmth in the room may also prove helpful in taming the excitement of the mind.

32 Post-meditation and subsequent attainment are both translations of the same Tibetan term, *jetop*.

33 Madhyamaka reasonings are based on the teachings of the Buddha found in the sutras, not on his teachings found in the tantras.

34 During which time the bodhisattva traverses the ten bodhisattva bhumis and attains buddhahood.

35 For a discussion of these latter two methods, see *Shenpen Ösel* 4, no. 3 (2000): 70-85.

36 One might wonder what is the difference between delight and misery and the kleshas or mental afflictions, since we tend to have desire for and attachment to delight and aversion to misery. The answer lies in the recognition that delight and misery are resultant states, feelings experienced as a result of virtuous and unvirtuous actions engaged in in the past, while kleshas or mental afflictions are the emotional motivations for the actions of body, speech, and mind that will ripen as results in the future.

37 Perhaps the most fundamental distinction that must be understood at the beginning of a true spiritual path is the distinction between secondary causes (Tibetan: *kyen,* here being translated as "condition") and primary causes (Tibetan: *gyu*). For any mental affliction to arise, there must be both a primary cause and a secondary cause. The secondary cause is that which we generally regard as the "cause" of our anger or desire or jealousy or resentment. It is that which, from the standpoint of the confusion of our dualistic clinging, we regard as the external event that is responsible for whatever our particular klesha of the moment may happen to be—whether that external event is the dastardly, inconsiderate, unthoughtful, and primitively aggressive blackguard out there in the external environment of our life, who does something intolerable that causes our anger, that, therefore, we are momentarily averse to, or whether it is the extraordinarily beautiful or handsome, and for the moment, considerate and elegant person out there that causes us to be dreamily in love. Regardless of the existence of those external provocations, for those confusing kleshas to arise, there also must be a primary clause, our actual actions in the past, and usually in past lives, that cause us to have the tendencies and proclivities to have these same emotions and to act upon them. The real culprit is the primary cause. The secondary causes are legion and not entirely under our control. The primary causes are our own creations, manifest only in our own minds, and, if we are willing to make the effort, the mental, emotional, verbal, and physical reactions that we have to the ripening of these primary causes, caused to ripen by the appearance of secondary causes, are totally under our own control. To give an example, if there is a plague, all people are exposed to the germs, which are contagious. But only some of them contract the plague. And why is that? Because, although all are subjected to the secondary cause, some people have the primary cause—their actions taken in past lives—and some have not. Therefore, some people fall sick and others do not. Similarly, some people who fall sick freak out, and others remain quite stoic or even at peace. Of a group of people who have all generated the primary cause of dying from the plague, those who have practiced no virtue as an antidote to that cause will die. Those who have practiced some virtue, may fall sick and not die, but may freak out and live the rest of their lives with impaired health. Others who have practiced more virtue may fall sick and remain stoic or even at peace. Others who have practiced even more virtue may fall sick, remain at peace, and recover entirely. And others who have practiced even more virtue than that may not fall sick at all. Ultimately, the cause is always within ourselves, as is the solution. "The fault, dear Brutus, is not in our stars, but in ourselves..." (Shakespeare, *Julius Caesar:* Act I, Scene ii). Of all the virtues that can be practiced as an antidote to the ripening of negative primary causes, the practice of vajrayana is the most powerful, the fastest, and the most efficacious.

38 Passion (desire, greed, lust, etc.), aggression (anger, hatred, resentment, etc.), ignorance (bewilderment, confusion, apathy), pride (wounded pride, low self-esteem, etc.), and jealousy (envy, paranoia, etc.). According to the teachings of the Buddha there are some 84,000 different conflicting emotions.

39 According to this presentation, the second instant follows so quickly upon the first that we are not normally even aware of the distinction between the two, but only perceive the second.

40 I.e., the four philosophical schools.

41 This seeing is not referring to the "seeing" described in the previous paragraph, but to ordinary, mundane seeing.

42 I.e., the buddhas.

43 Fixation here refers to fixating on aspects of experience as truly or substantially existent—to fixation on objects as existent, to the self as existent, etc.

44 Samsara is conditioned existence, existence conditioned by the fundamental misperception of the nature of reality that manifests as dualistic clinging and is of the nature of suffering. Nirvana is postulated to be the opposite of samsara–beyond suffering.

45 Relative truths in this context do not refer to codes of ethics or teachings which fall short of the definitive teachings of the Buddha, but which are somehow still useful to beings at various lesser levels of spiritual understanding. Relative truths here refer simply to what arises in our experience that is apparently real but not genuinely real.

46 According to the mahayana, there are five stages or paths that must be traversed to complete the path to buddhahood. These are the path of accumulation, during which the student is learning the dharma and engaging in meritorious actions which will gradually give greater and greater force to the student's practice of meditation and post-meditation; the path of joining or of juncture, sometimes called the path of application, during which the student's accumulation of merit and wisdom enables the student to meditate single-pointedly and therefore to go through and transcend all worldly meditation states; the path of seeing, which, in some descriptions, is the first instant of recognizing emptiness, which constitutes the beginning of the first bodhisattva level, and, in other descriptions, includes the first to fifth bodhisattva levels; the path of cultivation or of meditation, which again constitutes either the remaining nine levels or the last five levels of the bodhisattva path, during which the bodhisattva cultivates and expands the experience of what was seen on the path of seeing; and the path of no learning, which ensues upon the experience of the vajra-like or indestructible samadhi, the line of demarcation between the end of the bodhisattva path and the beginning of buddhahood.

47 The teachings on mind training. See Jamgön Kongtrül, *The Great Path of Awakening*, trans. Ken McLeod (Boston: Shambhala Publications, 1987).

48 The practice of sending and taking. See *Shenpen Ösel* 5, no.1 (2001): 62-70.

49 This term is often translated as "unbearable."

50 See *Shenpen Ösel* 2, no. 1(1998): 8:

> The nature of beings is always buddha.
> Not realizing that, they wander in endless samsara.
> For the boundless suffering of sentient beings
> May unbearable compassion be conceived in our being.
> When the energy of unbearable compassion is unceasing,
> In the expressions of loving kindness, the truth of its essential
>   emptiness is nakedly clear.
> This unity is the supreme unerring path.
> Inseparable from it, may we meditate day and night.

51 In any action, including actions which generate the accumulation of merit, there are three spheres: the doer of the deed, the doing of the deed, and the recipient or object of the doing of the deed. For example, in the practice of patience, there is the one being patient, the patience itself or the act of being patient, and the sentient being or event, such as the arising of anger, with which one is being patient. In the practice of patience as a paramita one seeks not to fixate on any of these three spheres— not to be acutely aware that it is I who am being patient and how noble I am for being so; not to regard the act of patience as something especially significant or worthy of notice or praise; and not to make a big deal of whom or what one is being patient with. Not to fixate on these spheres, but to see their true nature instead, prevents one from reifying them, from giving substantial existence to those things which in their true nature have no substantial existence. Ultimately, there is no self that is being patient, there is no act of patience, and there is no object of our patience. Not to fixate on these spheres, but instead to see their emptiness or to see them as the union of mere appearance and emptiness, is called threefold purity, and is that which distinguishes the paramitas—of generosity, manners and ethical behavior, patience, exertion, meditation, and prajna—from the ordinary virtues that carry the same name.

52 Abandoning that which needs to be abandoned and realizing that which needs to be realized in order to attain buddhahood.

53 Published under the title *Mahamudra: The Quintessence of Mind and Meditation* (Boston: Shambhala Publications, 1986).